100 Norfolk Churches of Village and Countryside
A Further Selection

100 Norfolk Churches of Village and Countryside

A Further Selection

Andrew Swift

Foreword by Richard Jewson J.P.
Lord-Lieutenant of Norfolk

First published 2017 by Velox Books
208 Milligan Road, Aylestone. Leicester LE2 8FD

Copyright © Andrew Swift 2017

Text, design, photographs and illustrations © Andrew Swift 2017

Photographs

Cover, Wickhampton St Andrew
Frontispiece, Paston St Margaret
This page, Chedgrave All Saints

ISBN 978-0-9575701-5-3

Produced by Biddles Books, King's Lynn PE32 1SF

Foreword by the Lord-Lieutenant of Norfolk

Norfolk is blessed by some 650 medieval churches, each one special and of interest, but altogether they form the character of our county. They affirm our long history and reflect the wealth brought to the county in the Middle Ages by wool and trade. Standing usually on the high ground they mark out our landscape. Andrew Swift is to be congratulated on providing an invaluable guide to 100 of them, including St Peter and St Paul in Barnham Broom where I have lived happily for fifty years.

Richard Jewson J.P.
Lord-Lieutenant of Norfolk

Introduction

What a pleasure it was to undertake the delightful task of immersing myself again in the evocative Norfolk countryside to visit, document and photograph another 100 of Norfolk's rural churches. This second volume follows exactly along the lines of the first one, and again is formatted to present the churches in as informative and approachable way as possible, without photographs split across pages and with each church entry occupying two facing pages for ease of reference.

Many of the salient points about, and issues affecting, Norfolk's village and countryside churches were discussed in the introduction to the last volume and nothing is served by repetition here, but a few things are worth reiterating. Firstly, an explanation of how the 100 churches were chosen. Two significant, fairly recent books by Tilbrook and Roberts (1997) and Stanford (2007) covered over 120 Norfolk churches, using excellent photographs and some description, and I was anxious not to retread the ground covered by the authors of those books. Also, the popular book by Simon Jenkins (2009) claimed to include the country's 1000 best churches, and those chosen for Norfolk (and everywhere else) are now on the 'Jenkins Trail'. There seemed little point in revisiting the undoubted merits of these churches, so they were also not considered. That still left an awful lot of churches, even taking into the equation the 100 chosen for my first Norfolk Churches book, so choosing another 100 for this book was not an onerous task. I maintained my policy of excluding town, city, overly familiar and celebrated churches, and also aimed for an even as possible geographical distribution across the county, which meant that several excellent buildings had to be left out. I remained committed to focusing attention on the lesser known and less often celebrated churches of Norfolk, and encouraging more people to visit them.

Happily, the move towards opening more churches to visitors is gaining momentum and more 'Church Open' and 'Welcome to our Church' signs are springing up. An awareness of the benefits of an open door is growing, and the buildings themselves become more alive with people in them. An unavoidable fact these days is that the small congregations of rural churches are often sorely taxed and sometimes unable to fund repairs and maintenance, and every contribution that can be garnered from visitors aids the struggle. In recent years much vital financial help has been made available by grant-giving bodies and government agencies, which has led to many churches being swathed in scaffolding, a very welcome sight, but all that could change. If our churches are to remain in good condition, then other sources of income must be found. Ultimately I believe that responsibility for the upkeep of churches should be taken on by the community at large. Ask the residents of any Norfolk village and most will admit they would hate to see their church fall out of use and become ruinous, even if they, like much of the country, are not churchgoers. That being the case, they should be encouraged to support their local church financially in some way, when help is needed. As in the first book, all but a few of the churches herein are regularly open for visitors, and the others are easily accessible via keyholders or churchwardens. Only two churches are not on the Church of England list of active churches, Dunton is maintained by the Norfolk Churches Trust, and Santon has its own Preservation Trust.

I am pleased to acknowledge the kindness and interest of members of the church family I have met on my travels, but especially those persons 'on the ground' in the individual parishes. These good folk form the bedrock of the Anglican church and without them the church as we know it would cease to exist.

Very sincere thanks go to Norfolk's Lord-Lieutenant Richard Jewson J.P. for his foreword to this book. Dr Joanne E. Norris once again helped in many ways to bring this book to fulfilment.

Andrew Swift
Norfolk
July 2017

The author at Ashby St Mary

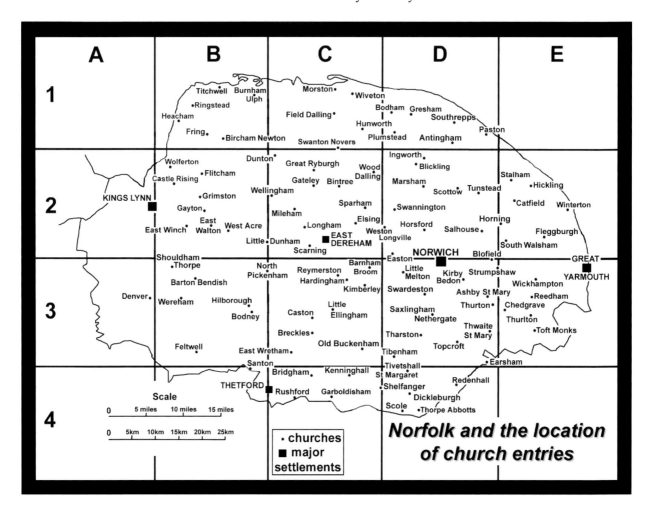

Norfolk and the location of church entries

All churches in the text are located by a letter/number reference on this map, also by ordnance survey grid reference.

The Churches

Antingham, Ashby St Mary, Barnham Broom, Barton Bendish, Bintree, Bircham Newton, Blickling, Blofield, Bodham, Bodney, Breckles, Bridgham, Burnham Ulph, Castle Rising, Caston, Catfield, Chedgrave, Denver, Dickleburgh, Dunton, Earsham, Easton, East Walton, East Winch, East Wretham, Elsing, Feltwell, Field Dalling, Fleggburgh, Flitcham, Fring, Garboldisham, Gateley, Gayton, Great Ryburgh, Gresham, Grimston, Hardingham, Heacham, Hickling, Hilborough, Horning, Horsford, Hunworth, Ingworth, Kenninghall, Kimberley, Kirby Bedon, Little Dunham, Little Ellingham, Little Melton, Longham, Marsham, Mileham, Morston, North Pickenham, Old Buckenham, Paston, Plumstead Redenhall, Reedham, Reymerston, Ringstead, Rushford, Salhouse, Santon, Saxlingham Nethergate, Scarning, Scole, Scottow, Shelfanger, Shouldham Thorpe, South Walsham, Southrepps, Sparham, Stalham, Strumpshaw, Swannington, Swanton Novers, Swardeston, Tharston, Thorpe Abbots, Thurlton, Thurton, Thwaite St Mary, Tibenham, Titchwell, Tivetshall St Margaret, Toft Monks, Topcroft, Tunstead, Wellingham, Wereham, West Acre, Weston Longville, Wickhampton, Winterton, Wiveton, Wolferton, Wood Dalling

Churches appear in the text in alphabetical order

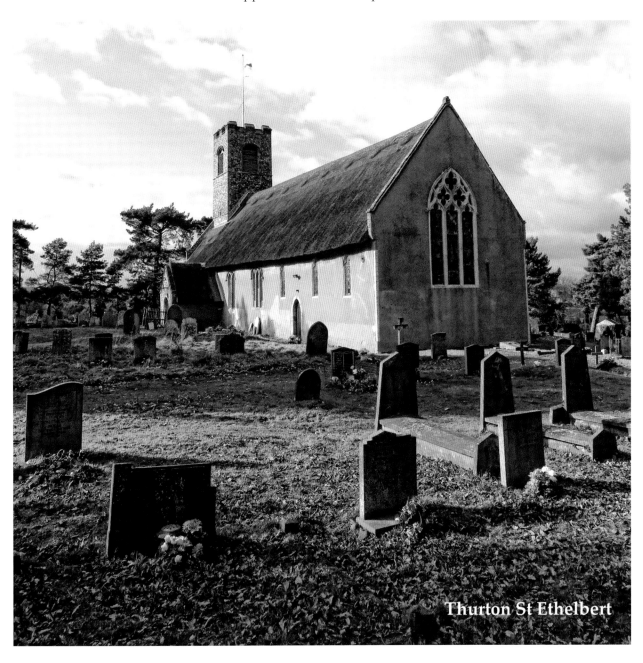

Thurton St Ethelbert

ANTINGHAM ST MARY

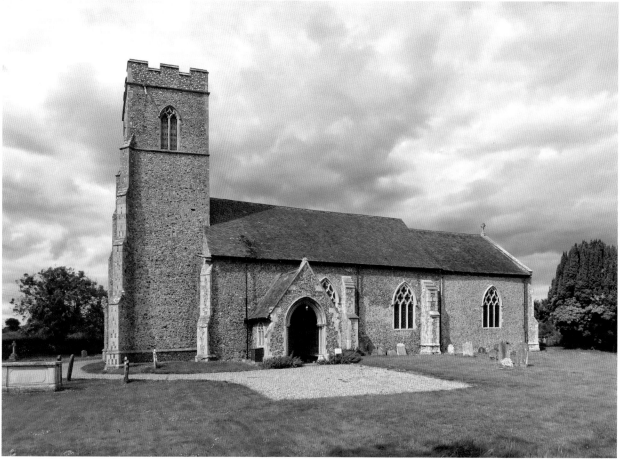

St Mary is largely C14ᵗʰ Decorated, but the top of the tower is Perpendicular

Antingham can boast not one, but two medieval churches in one churchyard. This is by no means a unique situation in Norfolk (e.g. South Walsham), and at Reepham there are three. One of the two Antingham churches, St Margaret, is a brooding, ivy-clad ruin, whilst St Mary remains as the intact, active church. Unfortunately, St Margaret is considered too dangerous to approach, but it is known from earlier studies that it probably began life in Saxo-Norman times. St Mary is later, being a largely C14ᵗʰ Decorated building, with the higher portions of the tower being of the Perpendicular period. Most windows are in the reticulated Decorated style. From the outside a clear structural demarcation can be seen between the nave and chancel, but inside that distinction is lost, except for different roofs. There are no aisles. Despite a thorough Victorian refurnishing in 1864/5 the interior retains several items of interest. The old C13ᵗʰ Purbeck Marble font is encountered as soon as the church is entered through the south doorway, and it is a familiar Norfolk type, with a shallow bowl ornamented with arches. The years have not treated it kindly and it is quite badly damaged. Near the font is a parish chest, certainly not as old as others in churches elsewhere, perhaps C16ᵗʰ or C17ᵗʰ, but a venerable survivor nonetheless. St Mary's stained glass forms a rather special assemblage of the work of some of the best designers and manufacturers of the Pre-Raphaelite school in C19ᵗʰ Britain. Two windows from the 1860's are by Morris, Marshall, Faulkner & Company and feature designs by Morris himself, Dante Gabriel Rossetti and Edward Burne-Jones. The Rossetti design of St Martha carrying pots and pans in the chancel south window may be his only work in Norfolk. The east window of 1868 is by King and Company; the chancel north window is later (c.1890) and is by Charles Kempe. There are several brasses in the church, some merely inscriptions, but the ambitious Calthorpe family brass of 1562 is noteworthy, not least for the plate depicting their 19 children! There are two medieval piscinas, the customary one in the chancel and one in the south wall behind the pulpit. Two fine wall tablets for John (d.1610) and William Kemp (d.1744) reside in the chancel, whilst on the walls nearby are two enigmatic stone heads. The rood loft stairs are still in place and open, but lead nowhere.

St Mary's tower · St Mary from the north · A very overgrown St Margaret

Looking east to west along the church · Looking east · Rood loft stairs

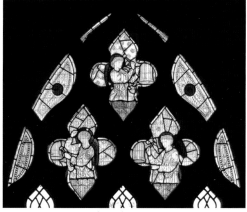

By Edward Burne-Jones · By Charles Kempe · Wall tablet of 1610 · The font

Calthorpe brass (1562) · Chancel piscina · Old chest · Two ancient figures

ASHBY ST MARY ST MARY the VIRGIN

St Mary the Virgin from the south

Charming St Mary in its serene setting is a pleasure to visit. Apart from the tall C15th tower, the aisleless building has its origins in Norman times, proven by two key features. First of all, the round-headed south doorway, which is a tour-de-force of Romanesque design and carving with several orders in the arch, all differently carved, and clustered piers with carved capitals forming the jambs. The doorway is in good order and has been protected for several centuries by the attractive south porch. This may be C16th and has a 'Tudor' outer doorway in brick. Secondly, there are two vertical courses of irregular blocks of ferrous conglomerate forming quoins in the nave walls, demarcating the original short Norman nave. The simple Norman church was enlarged in the C13th by extending the nave eastwards. In the south wall of the extension is a medieval priest's doorway. The lancet window to the west of this doorway is set quite low in the fashion of a low-side window. In the nave south wall is a memorial tablet of 1697 for Thomas Badley. 42 years later his wife's name was added. The largely pre-C19th interior is like a long hall, with no structural demarcation between nave and chancel. There are several appealing features. The small font near the south door with its long, fluted stem and shallow bowl ornamented with lozenges defies accurate dating, but is probably not medieval or Victorian, perhaps C17th or C18th. The neat cover may be later. Near the font is a characterful poor box and a substantial chest, probably of similar age. Immediately behind the chest, old wood panelling marks off the end of the nave seating. By the south doorway is an ancient, simple holy water stoup. The north doorway is blocked. The sturdy C17th wooden altar rails are beautifully-fashioned, with a fine gate topped by ball finials. In the east window is a small and easily overlooked foreign stained glass roundel dated 1604. The only other stained glass in the church is a representation of Holman Hunt's very familiar painting 'The Light of the World' in a south wall window. Although of common occurrence in churches, the quality of the Ashby example is very good. Two delightful gravestones for George and Ann Basey should be seen on the way out, to the left of the path. They depict their flocks of turkeys and geese.

From the west

St Mary from the north east

The south doorway

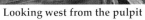
Looking west from the pulpit

The C19th organ, restored in 2009

Sanctuary and altar rails

The altar rails gate

Poor box, chest, panelling

The poor box

Lighting

The font, sealed north doorway

East window roundel

The Light of the World

St Peter & St Paul peeps shyly from its attendant wood

St Peter is a shy and retiring sort, and lurks amidst a screen of trees, with only the prominent tower on view, and even that is becoming surrounded. It's a shame because this C14th and C15th church contains some exciting items and deserves to be seen in its entirety, which would encourage more visitors. St Peter belongs to a group of 14 other churches, making it part of one of the biggest rural groups in England. North of St Peter are traces in the churchyard of another older church, St Michael, which was first consolidated with St Peter and then demolished in the mid-C14th. The first recorded vicar of the single living was in 1329. St Peter is an uncomplicated building, with a good-looking C15th tower with three Evangelist's symbols at the top (St Matthew's fell in the early 1990's and was subsequently stolen), C14th nave and chancel and C15th south porch. The north and priest's doorways are now sealed. The bottom stage of the tower has a decent west doorway and Perpendicular-style window, and the parapet boasts flushwork and shields on its battlements. All the church's windows were replaced in the C19th. The interior, though not extravagant, has some notable features. A big, early C19th west gallery looms over the nave and supports a rather grand organ. Mounted on the front of the gallery is a George III royal arms dated 1803, in very poor condition. Below the gallery is a strange font, the bowl resembling a castle turret. It may not be old, but the plinth it stands on appears older. Near this font are the church's two brasses. One of 1467 has a demi-figure and only half its inscription, whilst the other dated 1503 is largely complete; it depicts John and Ellen Dorant. In both nave and chancel most if not all of the roof corbels are old, and some are rather quirky, particularly a bovine head in the chancel with foliage issuing from its mouth, a sort of Green Bull. The C14th chancel angle piscina has blank shields around its two openings, a motif more usually seen in doorways. Beside it are drop-sill sedilia. Another piscina in the nave south east corner is associated with an aumbry, denoting that a side-altar once stood there. The rood screen is an excellent C15th example, with particularly fine tracery. The Saints on the dado are very faded, but can still be made out. In the north wall of the nave is the lower of the rood stair doorways, now blocked. The chancel houses a noble tablet of c.1680 for Gedding father and son.

From the west

Tower top stage

South porch and tower

South doorway

Interior looking west

Looking across the church

The screen

Screen detail

The chancel

Angle piscina

St Paul & St Peter in the chancel

George III royal arms

Brasses (1503 and 1467)

The font

Gedding tablet (c.1680)

Chancel corbels

13

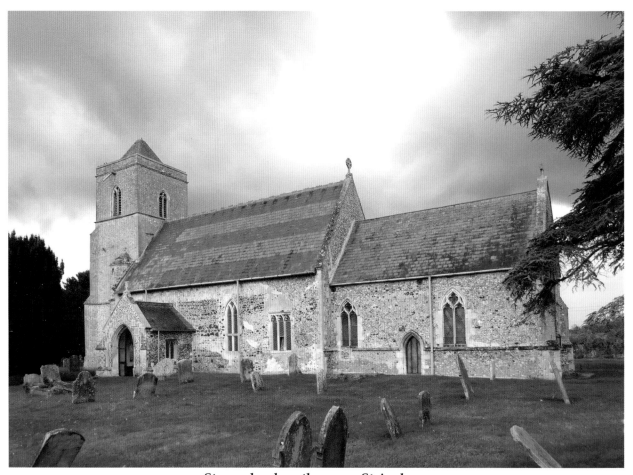

Storm clouds gather over St Andrew

Remarkably, there were three churches in Barton Bendish until 1787. All Saints was demolished in that year and its fabric used to shore up St Mary, and to mend local roads. St Mary was fortunate when the axe fell in 1974, and the building was passed into the hands of the Churches Conservation Trust. That left St Andrew as the last active church. The interior is rather dilapidated, but happily there are plans afoot for major restoration. The coarse and mixed fabric suggests early foundation and a Norman origin seems appropriate on the evidence of the south doorway, which despite what appears to be a later alteration to create a slightly pointed arch, has typical Norman motifs in the ornament. By its east jamb is an ancient holy water stoup, perhaps original. In the nave north wall are three Transitional or Early English lancet windows. The layout is basic, just west tower (with perky little pyramid roof), nave, chancel and south porch. The porch has an impressive flushwork frontage and an original St Andrew statue. The C14th tower has three cusped 'Y' belfry windows and one with Decorated tracery, renewed Perpendicular west window, west doorway with flattened 'Tudor' head and niches at the base of the buttresses. The interior initially promises few treasures, but investigation will be rewarded. The nave benches are intriguing, those on the south side are unremarkable doored, Victorian pews, but to the north is a super run of early C17th seating, with elegant carving on the sides and doors, and pretty knobs. A carved date of 1623 completes the picture. The octagonal font is plain and therefore difficult to date, but is probably medieval. A noteworthy survival up in the chancel is an expanse of small, medieval tiles in good order. Several designs can be discerned, some simple floral patterns but others have heraldic themes and more mysterious motifs. Not far away is a C14th piscina with intricately-worked head, with at its side plain drop-sill sedilia. In the floor beneath this piscina is a rare, earlier, double-drain piscina. The rood loft openings and stairs remain, and partly hidden by the pulpit nearby is an ornate C14th niche. Elements of the pulpit are C15th. Attached to the westernmost Victorian pew in the nave is an old poor box. Either side of the altar are indistinct, locally-produced paintings of 1884 which may be the four Evangelists, with angels above.

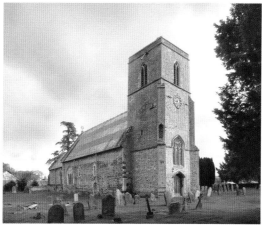

The south porch   St Andrew from the north west   The south doorway

Sanctuary and paintings   Looking west from the sanctuary   Piscina and sedilia

Rood loft openings, pulpit   C14th niche   Nave seating of 1623

Nearly 400 years old   The font   Medieval tiling

St Swithin from the north

Bintree St Swithin, in most respects, is a typical and unremarkable medieval Norfolk church, but like others of similar type, it has its own unique stories to tell, none more extraordinary than that of Father Richard Enraght who held the incumbency here for just three years from 1895 – 1898. It was his last post, for he died at Bintree and is buried in the churchyard. But before he came to the village he was at the centre of one of the most turbulent events in the history of the Anglican church. It is a long tale, but in essence, Fr Enraght subscribed to the tenets of the Anglo-Catholic Oxford Movement and was fervently dedicated to restoring pre-Reformation Catholic practices to church ritual. That brought him into conflict with the established church, which sought, in a very public and high-profile court case, to prosecute him for his stance. They were successful and he was sentenced to three years in jail, but only served 49 days due to the outcry that followed. The case effectively ended the attacks on 'Catholic' priests in the COE and helped establish the framework for the religious tolerance for which the modern Anglican church is recognised. A stained glass window of 1933 in the church celebrates Bintree's famous priest. The church itself is aisleless, but there is a large medieval south transept with an intricate Decorated south window (restored). The chancel has been rebuilt more than once since a fire in 1764. Its east window, in the Decorated style, has intricate tracery. Inside there are several worthy furnishings and fittings to admire. There are four floor brasses, three are simple inscriptions, but the other features a chalice. The C14[th] font on its two steps is a fine object, with Decorated tracery and other geometric designs on the bowl panels. Lurking against the east wall of the sanctuary is a rare, and unusually small, Norman pillar piscina. Of similar vintage is a short pier which for some reason was salvaged and reset into a window embrasure. The considerable parish chest at the west end of the nave benches is a formidable object, and may be very early, perhaps C14[th]. A distinguished chair in the chancel is dated 1664 and may be unique in featuring a Trinity design on its back. There are two good wall tablets, a formal memorial in white marble of 1842 in the nave, and a little further east, a rustic and characterful confection for Elias Brett, who died in 1739. The C20[th] Enraght window is excellent, and much of the C19[th] glass is also of good quality.

The church from the north west   ….. and from the south   Tower and porch

View east along the church   The sanctuary   The font

Two of the church's brasses   The parish chest   Norman pillar

Chair of 1664   Townshend tablet   Brett tablet   'The Enraght window'

17

Late November comes to Bircham Newton

A fascinating little church, All Saints is set on an exposed windswept site. An elusive and mysterious atmosphere surrounds the building, and its roots are very ancient. A Norman origin is confirmed by the round head and primitive structure of the chancel arch, also by the battered font. The windows are of lancet, Y- or intersecting Y-type, which points to most of the present building dating from the ?late C12th to the mid-C13th. The nave south wall shows a clear division into two building phases. There are no aisles or porches and the plan is very simple. The fabric is mixed and crudely-coursed, and there is a prominent stair turret on the south side of the tower. This is accessed inside by a low, narrow, round-headed doorway. The churchyard is quite large but most gravestones have disappeared, and the few that remain lean in all directions, reflecting the soft nature of the substrate. If the morphology of the church and its setting create a special atmosphere externally, then the interior is perhaps even more evocative. Everything gives the impression of being unchanged for centuries, there is almost nothing inside of even the C20th, never mind the C21st. An expanse of box pews with candle holders (there is no electricity) fills the nave, with a prominent bench end inscribed with the date 1858, but the benches have the look of older work. Perhaps the box pews were renovated in 1858. The pulpit could be C18th. An indistinct depression in the wall behind the pulpit may mark the sealed entrance to a vanished rood loft. The tapering, square font is a dilapidated Norman example and is still united with its original plinth. The highlight of the interior is the effigy of a priest located to the left of the chancel altar. Despite some wear, perhaps due to having spent some time outside, the preservation of the figure is good. Most of the interest focuses at the head end, where there is an elaborate canopy with the carvings of a sun and a child's face. Excavations beneath the effigy in the C19th revealed the presence of a child's body along with that of an adult, provoking intriguing questions as to the association of a priest and a child, which remain unanswered. Two old benches with poppyheads stand at the west end and three other things should be sought out – a George III arms above the chancel arch, the ancient piscina and an oval wall tablet of 1829 for a grandson of Admiral Nelson.

From the north west and south east

The south doorway

Looking east and west along the church

George III royal arms

Effigy of a priest

Chancel piscina

The font

The Nelson connection

Pulpit and box pews

Poppyheads of different ages

Doorway to tower stair

Blickling church from the south

It may be that only one visitor in 1000 comes to Blickling primarily to see the church, hardly surprising because only a short distance from St Andrew is the stunning C17[th] Blickling Hall. But if the visitor can tear themselves away from that fabulous pile next door, this is a rewarding church to study. Almost all medieval churches in Britain were overhauled and refitted by Victorian religious enthusiasts and their architects anxious to re-establish the influence of the Church of England via a programme of re-Gothicisation of its churches. St Andrew was thoroughly revamped, but whether its restoration was due to the fabric being in a poor state, for purely evangelical reasons, or that the family in the Hall wanted to smarten up the place, isn't known. Whatever the reason, St Andrew was almost entirely rebuilt by William Butterfield in the 1850's and G. E. Street in the 1870's. The sharp-edged C19[th] finish has mellowed with time, so today the church presents an agreeable picture. Some medieval work can still be identified, most obviously in the C13[th] south doorway and the somewhat younger blocked north doorway. The arcades and font are C15[th], as are the piscinas in the chancel and south aisle. The nave and aisle roofs are also old, but much restored. The nave west wall, including the tower arch and oculus window above, may also be medieval. The font features a pride of cheerful lions jostling for space, and lots of colour, while the aisle piscina (with wooden credence shelf) has a heavy, moulded arch. The chancel angle piscina is more exuberant, with sumptuous ogee arch and tracery over the main opening. The smaller opening also has a nice ogee arch and crowning the pillar between the two openings is a charming carving of a bird's nest with mother and babies. The interior is characterised by medieval brasses and later memorials, there are a large number of each. Several of the brasses have figures, the best being the large representation of Sir Nicholas Dagworth of 1401, with full supporting regalia. The one for Ann Wode, who died bearing twins, is most poignant, as she is seen holding the two babies. The memorial in the nave for the 8th Marquis of Lothian is arguably overly grandiloquent, but the tomb chest for Sir Edward Clere, the Elizabethan memorial for Eliz. Gurdon and the neo-Gothic gem for the 7th Marquis of Lothian in the chancel are top notch. The pulpit is a good Jacobean example.

Tower and porch   St Andrew from the north west   South doorway

Interior looking east   The chancel   Interior looking west

Pulpit, rood stair doorways   Chancel piscina   The font   Sir Nicholas Dagworth (1401)

Felthorpe (1454), Wode (1512), Boleyne (1485) brasses   Clere (1605), Gurdon (1582), Lothian (1841) memorials   Marquis (1878), & Marchioness (1901) of Lothian   Margaret Graile (1723)

Blofield church is dominated by its soaring 33.5m tower

In an area of generally unspectacular churches, St Andrew and St Peter is made of bolder stuff and proudly displays its grandeur to a wide area. This is mostly achieved by the magnificent Perpendicular tower, nearly 34m of it, one of the tallest in Norfolk. Its windows are large and extravagant, the parapet flamboyantly ornate, and at the corners of the battlements are stone figures thought to be the Four Latin Doctors. There is excellent flushwork at the base, the west doorway is super, the sound holes have a singular mesh design and to complete a most impressive ensemble Blofield's tower houses a regularly rung peal of eight bells. The rest of the largely early C15th building is scarcely less impressive, with two aisles, a large chancel and a grand north porch that previously boasted an upper room. The theme continues inside where there is a sense of spaciousness and richness, helped by the two soaring arcades. There is much to see but at first having entered through the north door, much is obscured by an unusual wooden screen dividing off the west end from the rest of the church. Immediately east of the screen there is a good set of raised C18th box pews and further east, many old benches with well-preserved arm rest figures and poppyheads. Most of the rest of the furnishings and fittings are Victorian, but the dado of a medieval chancel screen remains and retains much of its authenticity despite the panel figures being repainted. The C15th font was moved in recent years from the west end to a more easterly position in the north aisle, and is one of Blofield's finest treasures, due to the extremely rare carvings of scenes from the life of Christ adorning the bowl. The chancel houses a fine suite of wall tablets, dating from the C17th to the C19th, the most compelling is probably the tablet for Edward Paston and family of c.1630, but a plain tablet for the Rev'd Charles Reve, who died in 1727, holds more interest, for it was the good reverend who on his death left bequests which are still active to this day in Blofield as the Reve Educational Foundation. Also in the chancel is a good medieval angle piscina, and the C19th wooden reredos is ambitious and finely finished. The church's C19th and C20th glass is justly renowned and varied, and includes high-class work by the King Workshop, Hardman & Co, Kempe and Tower, and Reginald Bell. There are many other rewarding items to track down in this fine church.

From the west   From the south west   The tower from the south

View west from the altar   Screen and chancel   Looking east along the church

Angle piscina   Bench end figures   A selection of wall tablets

The font   Section of the screen   For Jean Parker, aged 10   Glass by Kempe & Tower   By J & J King

The church from the north west

There are two Bodhams, Upper and Lower, and whilst Upper is a lively small village, just off the busy A148, Lower about 1.5 miles south is little more than a very thin scatter of farms in a very rural setting. Yet it is in the empty spaces of Lower Bodham that All Saints is located. Being an isolated church confers the benefit of an invigorating atmosphere, and All Saints certainly has that. At first sight, the Decorated tower and Perpendicular windows suggest a conventional church of C13th-C15th age, but look closer, because the fabric here suggests a different story. It contains quite a lot of ferrous conglomerate, especially in the sliver of nave east wall lurking behind a buttress on the south side, where the chancel begins. Above the conglomerate courses the fabric changes markedly where later building becomes apparent. Ferrous conglomerate is a common feature in Norfolk Saxon masonry, but becomes very much rarer after the Conquest, so the inference here is that the small area of nave east wall is part of an original Saxo-Norman nave which later was largely rebuilt, but making some use of conglomerate blocks from the first building. Interestingly, the interior north doorway (now blocked) has a round arch, of Saxo-Norman affinity. The building continued to evolve as the years passed, and there are more tales here to unravel. The interior is plain and seemly, reportedly in recent times somewhat neglected, but now in good shape. There are few highlights, but amongst them is a rather spectacular pulpit, said to originate from a nearby workhouse. It seems to have been built of a set of parts acquired from various sources, probably in the C19th, including lovely turned balusters and linenfold panelling, some of which may well be pre-C19th. The open nave benches were also from the workhouse. The altar rails are a fine set, their balusters identical to those on the pulpit, and presumably from the same source. The font is plain and hard to date but damage on the rim of the bowl could indicate that a lock was once fitted, which would date it as medieval. The outstanding royal arms is for Queen Anne. There are two modest inscription brasses for members of the Fuller and Patton families. In a church of very few memorials, the Rev'd Norris, who died in 1832, is remembered on both a wall tablet and a floor stone. The nave piscina and two stoups, one by the outer south doorway backed with old tiles, are medieval.

All Saints from the south west and north east

From the porch

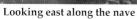

Looking east along the nave

The chancel

Nave looking west

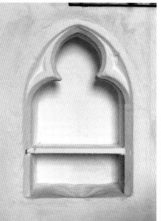

The font

Nave piscina

Stoup near south door

Norris family tablet (1832)

2 brasses & Norris stone

The pulpit, rood stair doorway

Altar rails

Queen Anne royal arms

25

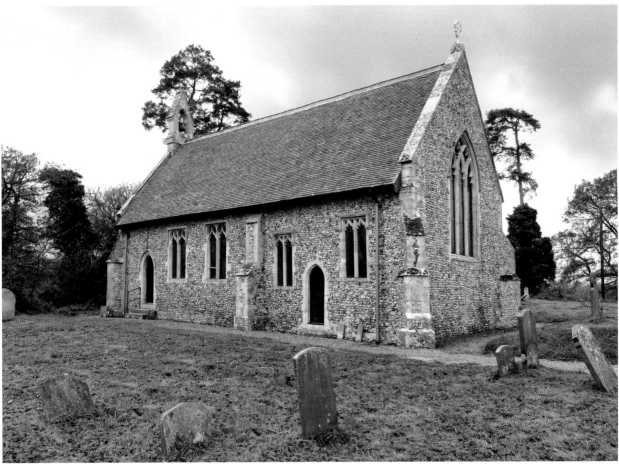

St Mary from the south east

The delightful small church of St Mary is easily bypassed, as it hides on a rise behind a screen of trees just off the B1108 road around 6km north of Mundford, and it's no use looking for the village of Bodney either, because there isn't one, just a thin scatter of secluded houses. But the finding is just one of the pleasures of stopping here and spending an hour in deep countryside appreciating a simple and homely little chapel. There are no great treasures here, instead a gentle serenity envelopes the building and its surroundings. Much of what can be seen today is Victorian, at that time the structure was rebuilt, all the windows replaced, and the little bellcote at the west end added, but it may be that St Mary was always just a single-cell building, with a foundation in Norman or perhaps earlier times. Yet there is a rectangular area beyond the east wall which shows clear evidence in the ground of wall lines indicating the former presence of a structure there. It has been suggested that this may be the site of an earlier church, but perhaps a former chancel stood here? The evidence for a very early origin rests on carved stones incorporated into the north east buttress, which are thought to be Saxon. Also, traces of a very narrow, round-headed, slit window, clearly early, can be discerned in the north wall, and inside the splay remains, now housing a modern statue. Some authorities claim that the large crude blocks forming the head of the C14th chancel piscina are also reworked from a preceding Saxon construction. The interior is simple and charming and first impressions suggest there may be little to interest the historian. But that would be misleading. The economy-sized font is the first item met with, and is a plain, tapering, octagonal bowl giving little away as to its date, but thought to be C14th. The nave benches form a pleasing set and have old, original backs with tracery designs, but other elements like the ends and poppyheads appear to be renewed. The Jacobean pulpit is modest but has a likeable panelled design. Near to it, both rood loft doorways are open, with stairs still in place, and the chancel arch bears the scars of the settings for the rood beam. In the chancel by the aforementioned piscina are drop-sill sedilia and, above them, is a consecration cross uncovered by the Victorians. Above the piscina is the head of an old niche or window. There are just two plain, late C18th wall tablets, for George and Teresa Tasburgh.

Old foundations and east end

St Mary under repair, from the north

The bellcote

Looking east and west along the church

The font

The sanctuary

Piscina, sedilia and consecration cross

Bench end

Traceried bench backs

Rood loft doorways, pulpit

Tasburgh tablet

Blocked window

St Margaret from the north east

St Margaret is a church with lots of 'feel', with one of the oldest round towers in Norfolk. It lies just off the B1111 road in almost complete isolation on the eastern fringes of the British Army's vast Stanford Training Area. Its village, apart from the odd farm, disappeared long ago, but there are traces in the large field immediately south east of the church which probably mark its site. The round tower has two clear phases in its construction, a lower three quarters which is dated, as so many are, as either late Saxon or Early Norman, but the tiny infilled circular sound holes have a very Saxon look about them. The topmost element of the tower is a pretty late C15th chequerboard patterned octagon. The tower arch inside the church is primitive and round-headed, with two moulded imposts bearing complex flowing patterns; these imposts and the basic form of the arch indicate at least a Norman date. The rest of the church is of modest proportions and plan, there are no aisles, but some imagination went into creating the reproduced Decorated and Perpendicular windows, particularly the east window with its flowing mouchette tracery. The interior reflects a very thorough Victorian refitting, but the historian need not despair, as there are several old items to track down. The square Norman font is a real gem, justly celebrated for its vigorous and varied carvings, which cover every centimetre of the bowl. As with many such fonts (*viz.* the Herefordshire 'school' and many in Cornwall) the subject matter is arcane and somewhat impenetrable. However, Green Men are one of the more obvious motifs and several guesses can be aimed at the identity of the figures beneath arcading on the east face; the carvings on the other two faces of the bowl are of a more obscure character. The C14th chancel screen survived the Victorian assault, in fact it was probably saved at that time by some judicious renovation, and a very fine one it is with notable flower carving and grand doors. In the chancel is a stately old piscina, accompanied by much plainer sedilia, the seats of which are almost at floor level, indicating just how much the chancel floor was raised in the C19th. Both rood loft doorways are extant, and a nice set of stairs rounds off a decorous feature. Above the tower arch are The Creed and Lord's Prayer from a set of boards, probably Victorian, while each side of the main altar are Ten Commandment boards, possibly from the same set.

Tower and porch   From the west   St Margaret's round tower

Looking along the church to the east   …. and the west   Sanctuary and east window

Tower arch, Lord's Prayer, Creed   Chancel screen   Rood loft entrance and stairs

Tower arch imposts   Three faces of the font   Angle piscina

There is much at St Mary to interest the connoisseur

The mostly C14ᵗʰ St Mary is a church with bags of character and mystique, features evoked in a fine 1989 painting by the artist John Piper. The exterior is idiosyncratic and the interior atmospheric. There is no tower, just a closed bellcote perched on the west end gable, but evidence on the intriguing west wall indicates the former presence of one, and judging by the narrow traces of where the tower abutted this wall, it was a round one. The blocked C13ᵗʰ tower arch fills the width of these ghost wall lines. Look closely at the wall to see lines of crude putlog holes extending across it. The Dutch gable is a C17ᵗʰ or C18ᵗʰ modification. The north porch is an odd beast, the tale of its evolution obvious in the very mixed fabric. The original C15ᵗʰ porch must have been a grand sight with lovely flushwork arcading all around, but at some stage it partially collapsed; instead of rebuilding it, the parish patched it up with flints and brick, and that process probably happened at least twice, leaving us with the quaint hybrid of today. The chancel stands higher than the nave, perhaps the latter was reduced in height when an earlier steep thatched roof was replaced. Walk around to the south side to see an excellent example of a low-side window. When curiosity has been satisfied outside, then more pleasures await within. An aura of antiquity and fading grandeur fills the air, and several compelling medieval features have survived the centuries. The august C15ᵗʰ font has suffered over the years but the features of the bowl panels can still be discerned, the most interesting of those bear depictions of the Assumption and the Trinity, both rare subjects on fonts. The dado of a rugged C14ᵗʰ screen still divides nave from chancel and original floral painting adorns the panels. Much C17ᵗʰ and earlier woodwork can be found in the vicinity of the screen, including a reading desk and large box-like pulpit, also a bench end of 1475 carved with text written in archaic English. Indeterminate fragments of C14ᵗʰ glass are collected in windows in the chancel. Also in the chancel are an exuberant double piscina and sedilia, both Decorated in style but clearly not contemporary. Across the tower arch are portraits of Aaron and Moses on board, the last vestiges of an old decalogue set. See also a much-weathered Norman font from ruined Roudham, a Norman pillar piscina bowl, a C13ᵗʰ bell, rood stairs, niches, box pews, a good early C19ᵗʰ wall tablet and much more.

St Mary from the north   External rood loft stairs   From the south west

Looking west and east along the nave   Chancel, screen, pulpit

Decorated window, piscina & sedilia   Rood loft stairs   The font   Reading desk

Bench end of 1475   Section of the screen   Aaron and Moses   C14th glass

The towerless All Saints from the south west

The Burnhams in North Norfolk are a churchlover's paradise, with no less than six active medieval churches within a very small area. Burnham Market is the largest settlement, but is actually a recent grouping of three villages, Burnham Westgate, Burnham Ulph and Burnham Sutton. Sutton church is now a sparse ruin, but Westgate and Ulph (Sutton cum Ulph after amalgamation of the two parishes) churches are both very much in business. St Mary at Westgate is larger, more imposing and looked upon as the chief church of the area, but All Saints is a worthy objective for the church explorer, and still boasts much evidence of its early incarnations. Externally, the slit window (with later trefoil arch) in the south nave wall, and another to the north with a rounded arch with dogtooth moulding, speak of Norman origins, and the arch of the blocked priest's doorway in the south chancel wall is also barely pointed and probably dates from around 1200. Another old window to the north has its arch made from what looks like an early tomb cover and below it is a conjoined low-side window. There may never have been a tower, for the bellcote is either C13th or C14th. The church is aisleless but has a curious porch, with two rectangular side windows with glassless, cusped, circular openings. More evidence for Norman origins can be found inside, in the shape of the chancel arch piers, which show a variety of waterleaf and other Norman/Transitional carving on the capitals. These were later cut through to accommodate the chancel screen that once stood there. The chancel arch itself is assertively pointed, and may be of later date. To its north the higher of the two rood loft openings is evident, but a little more effort is needed to recognise the lower one, because it is now converted into an image niche in a window embrasure. The C13th chancel piscina has suffered badly, but the ghost of what must have been a good ogee arch can still be discerned. There are no other medieval features, a pervasive Victorian refit left a bland set of furnishings and an uninspiring atmosphere. However, the C18th pulpit has survived from a Georgian furnishing scheme and across the other side of the chancel arch a nicely proportioned organ benefits from an uplifting white paint job. The font is a dull, generic Victorian model. A few old corbel heads enliven the nave roof, but almost all bear lugubrious expressions. Nelson's father was rector here in the C18th.

From the north east

The bellcote

Two venerable windows

The church from the west end

Organ, chancel arch, pulpit

West from the sanctuary

Chancel and east window

North east nave details

The pulpit

The font

Chancel arch details

Nothing to smile about

Niche, ex-rood stair opening

Chancel piscina

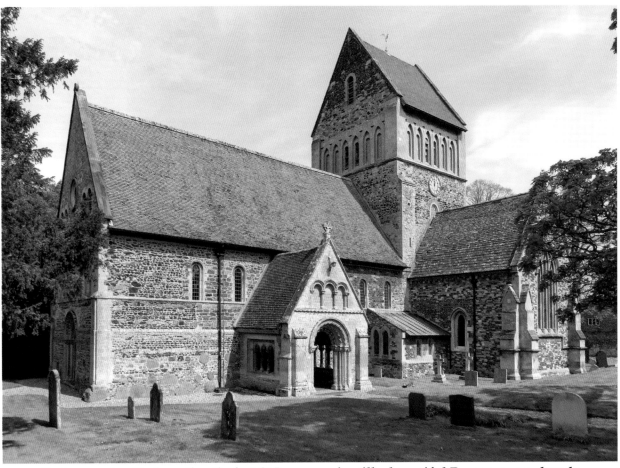

Perhaps not entirely authentic, but St Lawrence is still a beautiful Romanesque church

There is no doubt that St Lawrence is one of Norfolk's finest churches, but it is a building full of mystery and its evolution is still not fully decoded. It is always associated closely with the magnificent ruins of Castle Rising itself and the received wisdom is that the builder of that edifice, William D'Albini, was also the founder of St Lawrence in around 1180. And it is clear that a large part of the church is thoroughly Norman in appearance, but the walls of the nave in particular throw up a lot of questions. For a start they are very un-Norman in construction, with crude, haphazard coursing using stone of all types, shapes and sizes, suggestive of earlier work. Carstone, Silver Carr and ferrous conglomerate are the chief constituents, and at the base are huge boulders of Silver Carr, in places jutting out from the walls. There is nothing undoubtedly Saxon in the doorways and windows, but it can be seen in the nave that there are at least two phases of early building, the earliest seen in the blocked, simple round headed windows in the west wall and the oval window above, which are only seen inside. Further east the work is Late Norman and more embellished. Could a Saxon single cell church have stood here before the Normans arrived and renewed and added to it? The questions don't end there, but what is clear is that much Early English work followed in the C13[th], mainly in the chancel. Then in the C19[th] great changes were wrought on an apparently decayed building, masterminded in at least two phases by the architects Salvin and Street, who between them added a new top stage to the tower and south transept to replace one long gone. Street was responsible for the faux-Norman porch. However, the exterior west face of the church is a genuine Romanesque tour-de-force, all original except for the Victorian arcades and round window at the top. A tour of the interior is an exciting and intriguing exercise, there are Norman indicators everywhere, blocked arches and windows, round-headed doorways, groined vault to the central tower and grand arches into it, super C13[th] features in the chancel, which was much renovated in the C19[th], and much more. And there is the amazing font, said to have been rescued from an C11[th] chapel in the castle grounds. It is covered with sinuous and enigmatic carving, but three cats are evident on the west face of the bowl. St Lawrence is a marvellous church, don't miss it.

The porch

The west end

Detail of the west end

North doorway

The church from the west end

View east through the tower arches

View north from the transept

Chancel from crossing

The chancel

View west through the crossing

The nave looking west

Chancel arcade, piscina, sedilia

The font

Chancel arch, banner stave locker, tablet

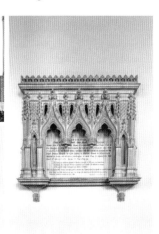
Victorian High Gothic

CASTON HOLY CROSS

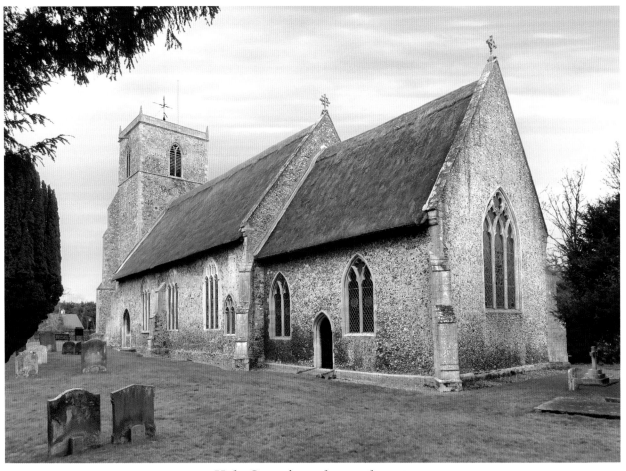

Holy Cross from the south east

West entrances through the tower add a touch of distinction to any church and the west doorway at Holy Cross, with its super ogee arch, is a fine way to enter this excellent church. But before entering the largely C14[th] and C15[th] building, a tour of the exterior should be taken, as there is much of interest. The south doorway is blocked and half-filled with a window, and has no porch, instead there is an impressive north porch, with parvise above, which was converted to a vestry many years ago. The all-brick construction and general architecture of this porch point to a post-medieval origin. After a period in the C19[th] and C20[th] with a slated roof the nave has reverted to a thatch covering, and most effective it is too. A low window at the east end of the nave south wall perhaps provided light for a chapel, and above it is a clearly ancient, blocked rectangular opening which probably lit the rood loft. Another blocked window can be seen in the nave north wall, and a little further east is a projection for the rood stairs. Beside that is a low window which may have illuminated a north chapel. There are no aisles, and the visitor through the west entrance encounters a long, barn-like nave, an impression heightened by the magnificent expanse of the roof, its C14[th] scissor-brace construction concealed beneath C15[th] chestnut panelling. The ribs are highlighted by painting and the bosses are gilded. More splendid woodwork comprises the early C17[th] pulpit, which may be the remaining portion of a triple-decker original. A number of bench ends, certainly old, but possibly post-medieval, are retained at the west end of the nave, these feature flamboyant poppyheads and lively arm-rest carvings. In the nave north wall is a medieval tomb recess, of modest design and now empty. The base of an old screen is still in place, it is restored and without painting, but set into the rear of the south section are two contemporary misericords, complete with carving on the underside of the seats. Nearby, an old bench is distinguished by C18[th] graffiti. Bombs dropping nearby in the 2nd World War shattered much medieval glass in the south nave windows, but fragments were later reset and there are several panels with figures. The plain font is probably C15[th]. A majestic C17[th] candelabra, said to originate from Hampton Court, hangs from the chancel ceiling.

The tower from the west

North side of the nave

The north porch

Looking east along the church

The east end

Looking west from the sanctuary

Nave south east details

Misericords and graffiti

Post-medieval benches and details

The pulpit

The font

Old glass

Arms of Victoria

All Saints from the north

Catfield lies in the midst of the busiest part of the northern Broads, and not far away is Wroxham, the unofficial capital of that region. The latter is choked with visitors and vehicles for large portions of the year, but Catfield remains a haven of peace and quiet more or less all year round, and thus has much to recommend it even before the fine church of All Saints is encountered. Much of the building is C14th, including the tower, nave and aisles, but the chancel is C15th. The south porch is imposing and has a slightly later parvise, reached inside by a super fairytale winding brick staircase. The south doorway has pretty fleurons, heads and shields around the hood mould, similar ornament also appears on certain arcade capitals. There are two aisles, each with a set of six large windows, four along the side plus one each in the east and west walls, all with striking tracery. The age of the aisle windows straddles the transition from Decorated to Perpendicular (i.e. from around 1340–1420), and designs characteristic of both periods are present. These big aisle windows compensate for the lack of a clerestory. The chancel windows are all Perpendicular, although the east window is very simple and is probably a C19th replacement. All the church windows appear to have been restored. Inside there is much to fire the enthusiasm of church lovers, and the list of worthy items is a long one. The medieval rood screen is very fine, especially the dado paintings, which unusually feature kings and one queen, many later canonised. The faces have all been attacked, but some, particularly those of the set to the north, are not badly damaged and features are relatively clear. The screen is the remaining part of one which used to run right across the church, on the evidence of steps and embrasures in aisle windows. The C15th font has an embattled rim, quatrefoils and flowers on the bowl and tracery on the stem panels. The faded and degraded traces of an extensive series of C14th wall paintings survive on the inner walls of the arcades, the best remaining are the stoning of Stephen and the ?martyrdom of St John Evangelist. The royal arms bears the lettering of Queen Victoria but the arms are of one of the Georges, clearly the panel was adapted for the later Queen. Across the tower arch are panelling and a door dated 1605, which may have started life elsewhere. There are a number of rather plain, but interesting, wall tablets in the chancel.

Tower and porch

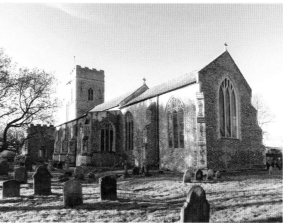

View from the south east

South doorway

Looking west from the sanctuary

East end of the church

Window and rood loft stairs

Steps to the porch parvise

The rood screen

Rood screen south side

Rood screen north side

Wall paintings - ?martyrdom of St John Evangelist, the stoning of Stephen

Font at the west end

Rebranded royal arms

CHEDGRAVE ALL SAINTS

E3, TM 363 994

From the southern churchyard

All Saints is one of those tantalising churches with a number of architectural oddities and conundrums. The setting is serene and attractive, but the church has a curious layout and looks as if it were built by committee. At the church's heart, the nave is unequivocally Norman, with one of the finest Romanesque doorways in the county (the north doorway is also Norman, but plainer), but the chancel is a C19th remodelling of a C15th original and the north aisle is a contrasting brick-built construction of 1819, extended to the west in 1993-4 in a similar style. Which brings us to the highly unusual tower, sited at the east end of the church to the north of the chancel. There are a few possibilities to explain this positioning, one is that it is the tower of a long-gone C12th church that ran off to the east, but there has never been evidence, whether on the ground, in the records or the fabric to suggest that was the case. Another more feasible scenario is that the bottom of the tower was originally a chapel running off the chancel, which was later raised to form a tower for housing the bells when the first Saxo-Norman tower at the west end (foundations for this were found when the extension was built) collapsed. Certainly the coursing of the tower appears to change around mid-height and the belfry windows have brick frames in the Late Perpendicular/Tudor style. The 'chapel' beneath is intriguing and has indicators of great age. It is at least contemporary with the nave, but may be even earlier. There are two small round-headed windows with double-splays, one to the east set in a curious round-arched niche and the other to the west has ancient intricate painting in the splay. Indeed, there are traces of original red painting throughout the chapel. Easily missed is a small, crude aumbry or piscina of keyhole form. The entrance from the chancel is round-headed. Together, these features point to a very ancient origin, maybe even C11th. Elsewhere inside, the chancel has an old piscina, and above it is a good wall tablet of 1694. Another oval tablet from around the turn of the C19th is quite plain. The east window glass is a montage of C16th and C17th panes from the continent, many in fine order and intensely coloured. Samuel Yarrington fabricated the window in the first half of the C19th, and it was restored by the King Workshop of Norwich in the 1960's. The C15th font features angels holding shields in the bowl panels.

40

The tower from the east

All Saints from the north east

South doorway

North doorway

Looking west from the chancel

The east end

A selection of glass from the east window

Chancel window angel

The font

Chapel window

Chancel piscina/Chapel ?aumbry

Webster tablet

St Mary from the south

For those used to the flint churches of the rest of Norfolk it comes as a bit of a shock to encounter the Carstone churches of the west of the county. They are not numerous, but the deep browns of this Cretaceous sedimentary rock are unmistakeable. The outcrop is very narrow and trends in a sinuous line from north to south from around Hunstanton in the north to Southery in the south. Carstone has been worked from Roman times as a building stone, despite its susceptibility to weathering. In places with better stone it would have been rejected, but here in Norfolk, any stone that can be utilised in building finds a use. Denver St Mary is built mainly of Carstone, and the stones exhibit all the colour variations characteristic of the series. The fabric contains a minor component of geologically much younger, dark brown ferrous conglomerate. The C13th tower is worthy of attention, as the coursing is very variable with both large and small blocks being used. There was a spire until 1895, when it blew down. Much of the rest of the church reflects a thorough restoration in the C19th, but two medieval niches either side of the east window and some lively grotesques were kept. The single north aisle dates from the restoration of the 1870's, as probably does the vestry located off the south wall of the chancel. The rather nice south porch has much older roots. The interior was refitted during the restoration and retains its Victorian furnishings and feel, but the nave roof, boarded in 1870, has character and individuality, and boasts what are thought to be original medieval bosses and shields along the cornice. Elements of the chancel arch may be medieval, but that too was remodelled. The chancel retains a medieval angle piscina and stepped sedilia. The unusual altar rail and well-balanced layout add to the agreeable character to the chancel. The font is also Victorian but is enlivened by attractive painting in the bowl panels. Several wall tablets with diverting inscriptions adorn St Mary. One of 1835 records the valiant and vain efforts of a seaman to rescue a shipmate, whilst others wax eloquent in prose and poetry about the virtues of the deceased. None are extravagant, but the tablet for John Dering (1836) has style and features a weeping lady. Most windows contain glass by Ian Pace, a pupil of Clayton & Bell, spanning a long interval from 1857–1904. A few benches have gnarled old poppyheads, which add character.

Looking towards the porch

From the west

Spirited grotesque

The view to the east

Attractive chancel

The view from the sanctuary

Glass by Ian Pace, c.1904 & c.1857

The painted font

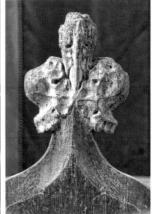
Old poppyhead

The nave roof

Nave roof details

Three wall tablets – late C18th, 1836 and 1789

Wooden eagle lectern

All Saints on a typical British summer's day

All Saints is a fine, large church positioned just off Dickleburgh's main street, and consists of aisled nave, chancel, south porch and small vestry off the chancel north wall. Some aspects of the building, like the unbuttressed tower, indicate C14th work, but many of the details are indicative of the C15th. The many handsome Perpendicular windows, including eight each side in the clerestory, have the depressed, 2-centred heads typical of the later part of that period. The showpiece of the exterior is the lovely south porch with its fine flushwork panelling, elaborate niches, battlements with quatrefoils and beautiful detailing in the spandrels of flowers, a jocular face and shields containing the symbols of The Trinity and the three crowns of the See of Ely. The interior is outstanding, with an extraordinary number of items and features of interest, despite an overprint of Victorian restoration. Starting nearest the south entrance we have a beautifully preserved C14th or C15th font, with woodwoses and lions on the stem, and angels and symbols of the Evangelists on the bowl, all in remarkable, undamaged condition. Behind the font rises a grand balcony on which stands an even more impressive organ, with pipes reaching almost to the ceiling. On the north wall a Charles II royal arms is affixed and above the south door are decalogue boards. The early C14th four-shafted arcade piers with their ornate capitals make an excellent show and lead the eye to a splendid cluster of items around the chancel arch. The pulpit is a showy, richly-carved C17th model with prominent bulbs and arabesques on the panels; just behind it the open mouth of the lower of the rood stair openings. The medieval screen (dado only) is most unusual and highly ornamented, with spirited and probably unique patterns based around large quatrefoils, the spandrels filled with a vivacious collection of men, beasts and symbols, all full of character and activity. The chancel houses three exceptional wall memorials, the oldest, for Francis Playters (d.1659), is a highly detailed piece featuring a demi-figure under a pediment. Only a little less imposing is a white marble tablet for Henry Turner who died in the Crimea in 1856, and the trio is completed by a High Victorian confection for Charles Turner (d.1854). All Saints boasts three medieval piscinas, the best of which, with ogee arch, resides in the south aisle. The substantial rood beam is still in place.

The south porch

View from the west

Chancel Priest's doorway

Looking east and west along the church

The west end

Pulpit, rood opening, screen

Screen panel

….. and detail

Curious old chair

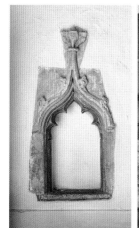

South aisle piscina

The font

Charles II royal arms

Francis Playters memorial

The church from the north west

The policy with '100 Norfolk Churches ....' is usually to exclude redundant churches, there were just two in book one, and St Peter at Dunton is one of only two in this second book, but St Peter has some special interest that merits its inclusion. Partly this is because this small aisleless church still sees occasional services (a policy of the Norfolk Churches Trust, who took over the church in 1978), but it also has one other feature that is unusual and worthy of wider attention. That is the presence of a bona fide rood loft, complete with functioning, open, original medieval doorways and stairs, meaning it can still (with care) be ascended and the chancel arch examined at close quarters. However, before anyone gets too excited, the loft itself is not medieval and is not even very old, around 110 years it is thought. But its presence gives a very rare opportunity to experience what a pre-1530's church must have looked like when rood lofts were in nearly every church. As a consequence of the Reformation and its aftermath in the reigns of Edward VI and Elizabeth I, almost all were taken down. St Peter was thoroughly remodelled in the late C19th and there is now little evidence to establish the origins of the building, but the blocked north door is from around 1300 and inside there are two intriguing and ancient carved blocks with heads at the corners, now used as mounts for reading desk and lectern, which may be older. What they were originally is harder to gauge. The windows are a mixture of Decorated and Perpendicular forms, with the oldest perhaps a nave south window, which has Y-tracery. However, it is probably not the original, so may be misleading. Not unexpectedly the interior is rather spartan, as befits a church that sees little use, but an inspection is not unrewarding. The plain square font is inscrutable and defies accurate dating, but may be pre-C16th. The tiling in the sanctuary is C18th, perhaps also the altar rails. The sanctuary side windows have been modified to form sedilia. There are several windows which contain Victorian glass of reasonable quality. Two of them, including the east, are by Heaton, Butler & Bayne and the sanctuary north is by Ward & Hughes. The piscina in the nave south wall is restored but is one of few remaining medieval features. Another is the pillar piscina in the sanctuary. There are two wall tablets in the chancel and a good 1st World War roll of honour in the nave.

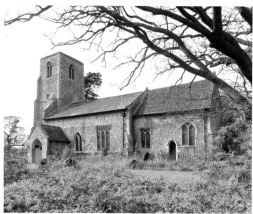

St Peter stretches out in the verdant churchyard | Tower west face | From the south

West along the nave | Looking east towards the rood loft | The east end

Sanctuary with pillar piscina | Rood loft stairs | William Case tablet (1857) | Roll of honour

Lectern base | The font | Nave piscina | Ward & Hughes stained glass

47

All Saints from the north east

Though common enough elsewhere in England, spires are distinctly rare in Norfolk, so the first sight of Earsham All Saints shingled example should delight East Anglian church enthusiasts. It is a nicely robust specimen, and looks just right, despite only being erected, it is thought, around 1700. Unusually, the original battlements of the tower are filled in and raised with brick, perhaps that occurred when the spire was erected. The tower is C14th and despite the prevalence of Perpendicular windows elsewhere, much of the rest of the church is earlier. The chancel has interior shafts to its windows which suggest a date around the turn of the C14th. The east window has reticulated tracery. There are hints in the fabric that the nave started life in Norman times, then it was lengthened and raised sometime after about 1350, probably when the Perpendicular windows were inserted. The north porch is C15th and has nice detailing around the entrance arches, and an arch-braced roof. The lack of aisles gives the interior a tunnel-like feel, an impression accentuated by the relatively long chancel. It is immediately apparent inside that this is a living church, with much evidence of the input of young people. The C15th seven sacrament font is somewhat mutilated as is usual, but much detail survives on the bowl panels depicting the sacraments; the eighth panel shows the crucifixion. The east window and two others house a splendid collection of C16th-C18th stained glass, both panels and roundels, brought over from the continent. The east window was probably assembled in the early C18th by Samuel Yarington from pieces imported by J. C. Hampp, and much of it of excellent quality. The importance of the glass is equalled by that of the wall tablets and memorials, which form a sumptuous assemblage, distributed around the church. Most are C18th and C19th memorials to the great and good. Notable among these are ones for Robert Gooch (d.1704), William Lamb (d.1724), Ann Windham (d.1762), John Dalling (d.1786) and William Windham (d.1789). Two box pews, one with opulent fittings, stand at the west end of the nave. The pulpit and reredos are excellent examples of Victorian craftsmanship and imagination. The west gallery is early C19th and may be ascended, with care, to give an overview of the church. The roofs are good, restored, C15th work. A large Hanoverian royal arms beneath the tower has been reported.

From the south

The north porch

From the north

Looking east over the nave

Chancel and reredos

West from the sanctuary

The pulpit

Box pew

Two east window panels

Nave window roundels

The font

Chancel piscina

Gooch tablet (1704)

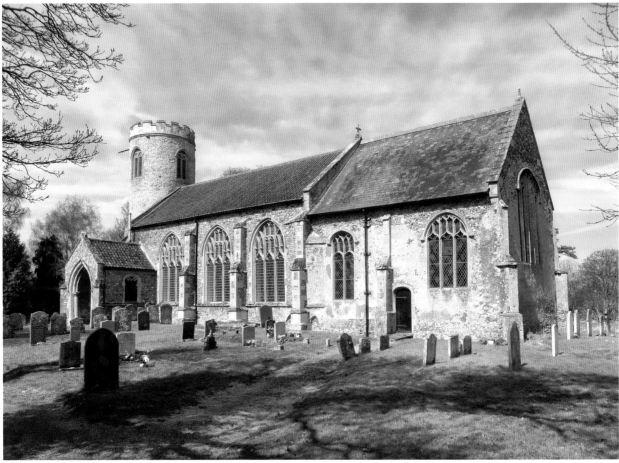

St Mary from the south

St Mary has an excellent C12th round tower with one small and one large lancet to the west, but attention is first drawn to the large and striking Perpendicular windows of the nave, which make a fine show. These and others in the chancel indicate a sweeping reconfiguration in the C14th-C15th, but clearly the church's origins are earlier. The picturesque porch with its crumbling window tracery is from around 1300 and the earlier of the two chancel arches (more on these later) is from around the same time. The inner arch of the south door has a round head and may be Norman. When a tour of the exterior is complete, cast a glance northwards to some ruins which are off-limits these days, but can clearly be seen. These are the remains of the ancient abbey chapel of St Andrew. The interior comes as something of a surprise in that it retains much material evidence of refitting and remodelling in the C18th. Not all of that was successful, a new lower nave ceiling was created which obscures much of the higher part of the western face of the chancel arch; at the same time the arch was largely filled-in and a new inner wooden arch erected. The end result was to leave only a small portion of the outer edge of the old arch and its admirable openwork foliage carvings visible. It is necessary to walk into the chancel to view the eastern side of the arch, which still shows the full extent of the outer edge carvings. When the C18th nave ceiling was fitted, the wall posts of the underlying, presumably medieval, roof were removed, leaving quaint head corbels marooned on the walls. Some box pews in good preservation remain from the C18th refit at the east end of the nave, and on the south side these are united with an excellent triple-decker pulpit. From earlier times comes the tapering, octagonal C15th font, which has quatrefoils on the bowl. Also from the C15th comes the small inscription brass of 1490 in the nave floor before the chancel arch. This asks us to pray for the souls of William and Margaret Baker. The priest's doorway in the south chancel wall has a very curious tympanum, of triangular form and featuring a large flower surrounded by fluid carving. While there is no evidence to prove it, the tympanum appears to have been remounted here from elsewhere. On the west wall is a good example of a George III royal arms, which by its devices can be dated to before 1801. In the chancel is an unusual square piscina, also drop-sill sedilia.

St Mary from the north east

.... and from the south west

The ruins of St Andrew

Looking west past the box pews

View across the nave

The chancel

Box pews and pulpit

Priest's doorway

Lemon wall tablet, early C19th

The font

George III royal arms

Head corbel and inscription brass

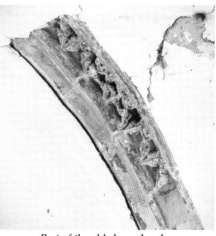

Part of the old chancel arch

All Saints from the south east

The churches of west Norfolk generally have a quite different look and feel to them than their contemporaries further east. This is due to the geology, which dictated what sort of stone was available for their construction. In west Norfolk a sandy brown, rather soft iron-rich sandstone crops out, called Carstone; it is around 107 million years old. Often to be seen in the same buildings, particularly churches, is a very similar stone, a dark, purple-brown, ferrous conglomerate, which is much younger, a matter of thousands rather than millions of years old. Both types of stone are seen at East Winch, with some flint too. The conglomerate is often stated to be an indicator of very old churches, so its presence here might suggest an ancient foundation. There is no unequivocal, original pre-C13th fabric, but inside is a Norman pillar piscina, so there may have been an early church here. Most of what is seen today is C14th-C15th with much Victorian restoration by Sir Gilbert Scott. All Saints has two aisles, a sanctus bell turret and a nice Tudor brick porch with insets of flint flushwork. The south door is C15th, as are the roofs inside, with various degrees of restoration. The C19th south organ chamber stands on the footprint of a medieval chapel, while on the opposite side of the chancel vestiges of an arcade in the wall show that a chapel also once stood to the north. Inside, there is a miscellany of surviving features including a C14th font with shields and foliage on the panels and a super Comper cover of 1913, part of the old rood screen, two medieval coffin lids, one probably associated with a mason, an obscure George III royal arms and a few fragments of old glass. In the chancel are two small hatchments and several wall tablets. The best of the latter, dated 1670, is for Owen Barnes. Another Barnes tablet of 1657 is almost hidden by the organ. The aisles are filled with hoary, silvery C15th benches; better preserved old bench ends were reused at the front of the nave. A few of the battered benches have much-abused arm rest figures but the bench ends at the front have better preserved examples, including mythological creatures. Some or all of these may be Victorian in origin. C19th glass of variable quality fills several windows. At the west end are an old chest and bier. The chancel medieval piscina and sedilia are unadorned. C15th corbels support the nave roof. Either side of the altar are impressive, ornate lamp holders.

Tower west face

Church from the south west

Porch window

South aisle head stop

Interior looking east

The chancel

Interior from the sanctuary

Screen, pillar piscina

Sanctuary south east

Medieval benches, arm rest figures

Font and cover

Tomb covers

Barnes tablet 1670

Chest, bier

53

EAST WRETHAM ST ETHELBERT

A pleasing prospect, St Ethelbert from the south

Lovely St Ethelbert is not old, being rebuilt almost entirely by Richard Armstrong in 1864-5, but other buildings have stood here since at least Norman times, and surviving from an early church is the Romanesque south doorway, with varied mouldings in the arch, and waterleaf capitals. Lower parts of the tower are also Norman, but the saddleback roof dates from the rebuilding. The C14th tower arch remains from the last medieval building. The rector at the time of the rebuilding, Rev'd Whalley, was heavily involved in every aspect, particularly the building of the chancel, and meticulously recorded the progress of the works. The excellent church guidebook contains excerpts from his account. His name in flushwork can be seen on an east wall buttress. Another dedication to the rebuilding, recording the role of the Wyrley Birch family from Wretham Hall, can be found on the tower west wall. The agreeable churchyard contains war graves of Czech and Polish airmen. Yearly services at the graves are well-attended, and representatives and relatives from the two countries are often present. The interior is delightful and is a fine illustration of Victorian religious sensibilities, and is still in its almost original 1865 state. Rev'd Whalley had a big input into the decoration and fittings, and taking inspiration from Rennaissance Italian artists, he created the murals on the chancel walls and in the window reveals. He also painted the organ and font cover, the latter alone took him 18 months! The design of the angle piscina in the chancel, with attractive vine carving above, echos the C13th original that preceded it. Beside it are drop-sill sedilia. The superb font cover was created as a smaller copy of Elsing's magnificent edifice, and quite overshadows the ornate font beneath, itself a not inconsiderable item. The arcade capitals have pretty waterleaf carving. The rest of the Victorian fittings are excellent, and the handsome carved, wooden reredos was installed in 1928. Glass by Powell & Co, and Clayton & Bell adds to the engaging ambience. Two pre-C19th features, a simple wall tablet of 1787 in the tower room, and a stained glass Elizabeth I royal arms in the vestry, are worth seeking out. 20 year old 2nd Lieutenant Noble, killed in the 1st World War, is commemorated by his battlefield cross and a large, distinctive memorial by Lutyens. Near to the latter on the nave south wall is another expansive wall memorial.

St Ethelbert from the west and north west

The Norman south doorway

The interior looking east

The chancel

Sanctuary south east

The reredos

Sanctuary details

Font, cover and arcade

The organ

Elizabeth I royal arms

2nd Lieu. Noble (inset), his battlefield cross & memorial

Easton St Peter and milepost

When St Peter was first built in at least Norman times, and until the C19[th], Easton would have been a workaday little village which probably congratulated itself inwardly that the wicked city of Norwich was a comfortable distance away. Now it looks nervously to the east as the city presses ever closer, and these days Easton consists largely of dormitory housing, with a lot more coming soon. The old milepost that miraculously still stands outside St Peter's gates is a reminder that once, 6 miles was a long way away. Yet around the old church on the western edge of Easton, a faint whisper of the old village persists (if it can be heard above the roar of the A47 nearby), and will do until the houses finally overtake it. The tower fell in the late 1700's and no-one bothered to clear up the rubble, and it can still be seen in sad heaps by the west wall. The nave to the south has unsightly rendering, but the much rebuilt, once two-storey porch, with a sundial bearing the date of 1694 and a very mixed fabric, is full of character and houses a real treasure, a fabulous Norman doorway, heavily enriched with carvings both familiar and obscure. The arch of the doorway is now somewhat pointed, but was clearly originally round, as the spacing of the wheel carvings goes awry at the top as a result of the modification. The interior is an interesting mix of ancient and modern. At the west end is a modern room at the level of an old style gallery, reached by stairs, also a new kitchen and toilet at ground level. The individual seats in the nave and aisle are also of recent origin. Yet, laudably, the old pamment tile and ledger slab floor in both areas has been retained. There are several other older features and fittings, the first one to be met with being a familiar C13[th] Purbeck Marble font, of typical form with twin arches on the bowl panels. On the walls are a few good memorial tablets, although they are not in the best condition. Two are worthy of note, a flamboyant but very badly faded cartouche with cherub and urn from ?1712, and a white marble tablet for Philip and Elizabeth Vincent of the 1720's. The pulpit is a superb C16[th] example with linenfold and tracery panels on baluster legs, with an hourglass stand attached. In the east window is a well-preserved, continental roundel of the Crucifixion, C16[th] or C17[th]. A small inscription brass is set in the nave floor. There are some old poppyheads in the chancel, also a plain piscina and sedilia set.

From the south west, with tower remains

St Peter from the north east

North doorway

Interior looking east

The chancel

Looking north west

Chancel south east

The pulpit

Old bench

Crucifixion roundel

Hourglass holder, 2 wall tablets

2 corbels and a brass

The font

Piscina, niche, ledger slab

57

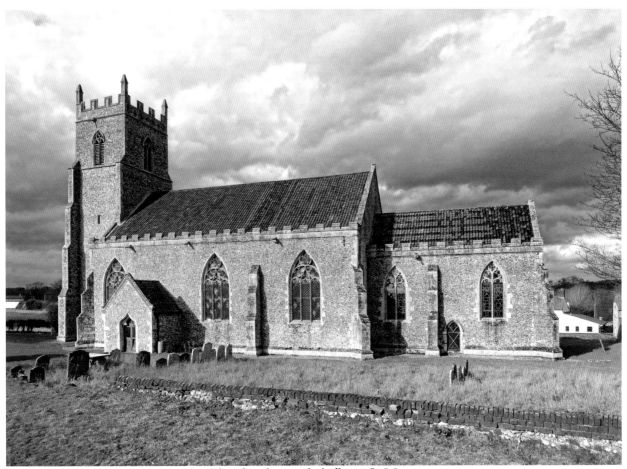

The clouds part briefly at St Mary

Although a great number of Norfolk churches were built in the days preceding the Perpendicular period, not many remained unchanged after it, such was the intensity of the remodelling and augmentation that characterised that period. There were some exceptions and St Mary at Elsing is one of them. This is a church almost entirely of the Decorated period, built in one programme in a relatively short time around 1335. The windows are especially notable and contain beautiful examples of flowing Curvilinear tracery. The two porches have ogee arched outer doorways and the north inner doorway has an impressive ogee arch too. The nave is of quite exceptional width and is one of the widest in the country, giving an almost cathedral-like airiness to the interior. Existing documents record that Sir Hugh Hastings was responsible for commissioning St Mary to replace an older church that stood on the site. A small area of walling remains from that early church in the west wall of the nave, south side. Sir Hugh was clearly an influential and powerful man and ensured that when his time came, he was interred in the floor of the chancel with a quite magnificent brass over the grave. Many such brasses were lost in the years since, usually stolen for their metal, but Sir Hugh's brass has survived, albeit in a depleted state. Yet it remains a magnificent and important object, reset now on a plinth in a central position in the chancel. Nearby is a tomb chest from 1623 for Dame Anne Browne, with black marble lid and a black-letter inscription on the wall behind. The chancel south east and south west windows contain some remarkably intact medieval glass figures of Apostles, together with some other figures. Unfortunately, some Apostles faces are incomplete or obscured by chemical darkening. In the east window a few fragments of old glass are gathered. The elegant font may be contemporary with the church, but it is its magnificent restored C15th canopy that steals the show. The dado of what must have once been an impressive medieval screen extends across the chancel arch. Restoration revealed figures on the panels, and allowed the identification of some interesting subjects, but even after this rehabilitation, the figures remain very indistinct. The C14th piscina and sedilia in the chancel form a fine set. Above the south doorway are a respectable royal arms for George III. Many substantial ledger slabs are set in the chancel floor.

St Mary from the north | North porch and tower | From the south west

North doorway | Looking east and west along the nave | The east end

Chancel piscina and sedilia | Font and canopy | Two panels of the screen dado | Disgruntled donkey

Dame Anne Browne's tomb | Hastings brass (1347) | George III royal arms

St Mary in high summer

South west Norfolk is close and secretive, the population small and scattered, and the empty flatlands of the Fens begin on Feltwell's western edge. The area is very distinctive, and looks and feels completely different from the rest of Norfolk. It is just the sort of place to find an intriguing and slightly mysterious church like St Mary. There is little doubt that if transported to the tourist hotspots of The Broads, this church would be much better known, as it has many treasures within. The building is very long, made so by the lengthy chancel, suggestive of C13th origins. The south aisle is very narrow, which again is often taken as a C13th indicator, while the bold north aisle, under a gabled roof, is clearly Victorian. The chancel east window is flowing Decorated, the side windows reticulated. The south aisle windows are Perpendicular, but may have replaced earlier ones. The south porch is late C13th or early C14th on the evidence of the windows, and is notably deep, with much roughly dressed limestone in its fabric. The tower is impressive, especially the tall pinnacles, stepped parapet and flushwork panelling at the top. Inside there is something rather special, a nave full of opulent C15th benches, with beautifully worked backs and fine ends with poppyheads, figures and animals. The latter fell foul of the wrecking crew, but some important carvings escaped and others were left recognisable. The Decorated south arcade has handsome capitals. The splendid and intricate nave roof is C15th and has retained its beam-end and, to the south, wall post figures. These are shield-holding ?priests and white-painted demi-angels. The cross beams also bear angel carvings and the spandrels have delicate tracery. The south aisle roof also contains good work. Some C15th elements lurk in the extravagant rood screen, but it looks very much what it is, Victorian. The entrance and stairs to the old loft still exist at the east end of the south aisle. The other great treasure of St Mary is the C19th stained glass in the chancel; this was made in C13th style by two renowned French artists, Oudinot and Didron. The colours are intense and beautiful. Two nicely-preserved old brasses are mounted on the chancel south wall, one in a sedile recess, and nearby are two superior wall memorials for Moundefords of 1580 and 1590. The piscina and sedilia set is eye-catching and the C19th font beautifully made.

St Mary from the south west and west   South porch

South east across the nave   The rood screen   Nave roof   Nave roof figures

French glass; Hecht, Mundford brasses   South west across the nave   Bench end burial scene   Checking the prisoner!

Chancel piscina and sedilia   Rood loft access   The font   Moundeford memorial (1580)

61

St Andrew from the south west

The largely C14th-C15th St Andrew is a real explorer's church, with fascinating details both inside and out. It consists of west tower, nave, north aisle, chancel and south porch. A wide arch and associated doorway in the chancel north wall, both blocked, once opened onto a north chapel. There was only minor reconfiguration in Victorian times, ensuring that the church of today retains its strong antique quality. A predominance of Decorated characters in the windows of the chancel indicate a C14th origin, but elsewhere there are bold Perpendicular windows in the nave from somewhat later. The arcade is C15th and very elegant. Recent expert investigations suggest that a small Norman church stood on this site. These revealed details in the masonry of the aisle north wall of Romanesque character, including a line of quoins to the east of the existing north door, a blocked doorway further east and a stone head possibly originally from a corbel table. It seems likely that the aisle north wall was the north wall of the Norman church, with the long demolished south wall located to the south of the present arcade. A round tower may once have stood where the westernmost bay of the aisle now stands. Inside there is much to see. The font is C15th and stands on a rugged base that may be older, the bowl panels are ornamented with an intriguing variety of motifs, including instruments of the Passion, a St Andrews Cross, Trinity symbol, etc. The font cover is a sturdy Jacobean example. In the chancel is a simple, but attractive C14th angle piscina and associated drop-sill sedile. Three inscription brasses are set into floor stones, one dated 1485. Some good, if rather murky, medieval glass is mounted in the tracery of several nave windows. Much of it depicts Saints, including a good set of female representatives, also Apostles, Prophets and angels. Many of the medieval figures are augmented by later glass, and several figures are entirely of recent (probably Victorian) origin. Some fine Victorian glass by Warrington can be seen in the east and other windows. The excellent arch-braced nave roof is C15th, as is the aisle roof. The nave seating is mostly medieval with poppyheads and later backs, and there are four rickety box pews of two types. On the aisle north wall is an indistinct wall painting, showing a tree and birds, possibly a Garden of Eden scene. A pre-1801 Hanoverian royal arms is mounted above the north doorway. Old chest under the tower.

The church from the north east and west

Preaching cross

Views towards the east and west

Nave seating

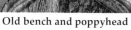

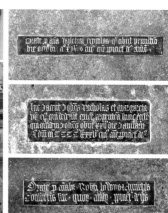

Old bench and poppyhead

Angle piscina

The font

The three brasses

Hanoverian arms

Wall painting

C14th glass

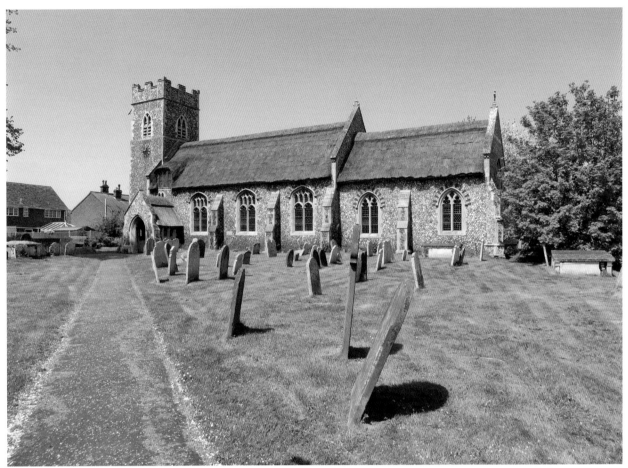

A charming scene – St Margaret from the approach path

Fleggburgh, also known as Burgh St Margaret, is the 'capital' of a romantic and mythic area known as 'The Flegg' or Flegg Island, which once stood up as an island in the midst of a large estuary. It is thought to have been a Danish stronghold in early medieval times. Even today, a detached and slightly otherworldly air suffuses the area, and St Margaret is off the church tourist map, which is a shame, for this is a trim and likeable church. It will soon be even more neat and tidy, for the church has secured a substantial grant towards new thatch (St Margaret is one of only 53 overall thatched churches in Norfolk) and other renovations and improvements. Despite its C14[th] origins, St Margaret appears to be more a C19[th] building, as a result of pervasive restoration and refits during the latter part of that century and into the C20[th], which removed most of its old features and fittings. But there are two remaining features which tell of a church that stood here three centuries before the C14[th]; one complete doorway and one part doorway. The south doorway is coarse Norman work, heavy and solid in the round head where there is billet and zig-zag work. There are two shafts each side. All that remains of the corresponding north doorway is the outer moulding of a round arch, with billet-work, and even that may be reset. The interior is small and intimate, there are no aisles or other extensions. The font of 1876 is assertively carved in an expressive Gothic mode, with IHC, floral and foliate motifs. At the west end stands a bold balcony, originally seated, now used as a meeting room. It is lit from the outside by a pretty dormer window above the porch. There are modern brasses for past rectors, their families and other worthies, and wall tablets from the C19[th] and C20[th]. The best of these is for Captain George Fisher who was killed near Gaza in 1917. It was erected by his father, the Rt Rev'd George Carnac Fisher, who held many prominent positions in the Church of England including Bishop of Ipswich; he died at Fleggburgh in 1921 and has a brass in the church. One much older brass has survived, mounted on the south chancel wall and dated 1608; it is for Joannes Burton. The marble reredos is a handsome example, given by Bishop Fisher. The east window has striking modern glass by Paul Jefferies. The Creed and Decalogue tablets nearby are supported by old corbels. One of the nave roof bosses is a mythical, 'dragon-bat' creature.

St Margaret west end

From the north east

Norman south doorway

Looking east

The east end

West from the sanctuary

The west end and balcony

Creed and Decalogue panels

Burton brass (1608)

Modern Fisher-related brasses

For Cap'n Fisher (d.1917)

The font

Eagle lectern

East window

The 'dragon-bat'

St Mary from the south east

St Mary has a long and fascinating tale to tell, and visitors who enjoy a bit of sleuthing will find much to divert them here at Flitcham. To begin with, the exterior is puzzling. Conventionally, a church tower is located at the west end, so it is logical to assume that is the case here, but it is not. A compass (or a quick peek inside) will establish that the tower is at the east end. Then there is the ruined south transept running off the tower, and raised plateau beyond it to the east. At some point it becomes apparent that the east tower once had a chancel running further east (the raised plateau marks its extent) and that the tower was a central tower. Furthermore, the south transept would be one arm of the cross of a cruciform church. There is no trace of a north transept but it is logical to assume that one once existed to complete the ground plan of a cross. The whole thing becomes easier to understand when the tower itself reveals itself to be Norman, evidenced by the blank arcading in the middle section. The Normans were fond of their cruciform churches. Losing the chancel of a cruciform church presents problems, i.e. what to do about the sanctuary and altar. The solution here was to convert the base of the tower to a sanctuary and to squeeze the essentials of the holy east end into the small space there. It is safe to say that the sanctuary of St Mary is snug. The old Norman tower arch to the west was retained to become a chancel/sanctuary arch, and its Romanesque character can still be appreciated. An odd large piscina was inserted into the north wall of the sanctuary, perhaps it was the original from the demolished chancel. There is evidence of Norman windows in the nave and tower. The rest of the church holds no great treasures, but it does contain lots of evidence of the patronage of the royal family in the late C19th and C20th. Sandringham is nearby and the royals have consistently taken an interest in their local churches. The ornate C19th font, via the agency of Prince Edward, arrived from Sandringham in the 1880's, and he, when king, provisioned the seating in 1907. The angels on the nave east wall holding texts from a hymn are also from Sandringham. Much general restoration was also sponsored from Sandringham from around 1880 and the interior as a result contains few old items and is overwhelmingly Victorian/Edwardian in feel. However, an inscription brass from 1614 has survived.

Ruined transept and tower
St Mary from the north east and east

Looking east and west along the church
The sanctuary

The arcade
Chancel arch from the east
Pulpit and reading stand
Sanctuary piscina

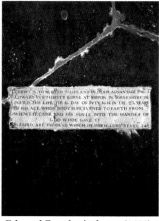

The font
Edward Runthwitt brass (1614)
Angel wall plaques
South doorway

67

FRING ALL SAINTS

All Saints southern aspect from the approach path

The tiny village of Fring is secreted in the gentle wolds to the south east of the 'seaside coast' around Hunstanton. This thinly populated area, though well husbanded and converted efficiently to the needs of modern farming, retains a mysterious, primitive atmosphere. Walks through this landscape take on an otherworldly air, and the paucity of settlements only intensifies that sensation. And in the midst of it all, as if it has stood there for ever, is All Saints, alone and enticing. The mostly early C14th building is not grand or full of treasures, but it does offer a number of diverting features, and it is clear that many changes have been wrought here over many hundreds of years. Externally there are several blocked openings, including doorways, windows and a low side window in the chancel south wall, and the tower has a curious lozenge window in its lower west face, restored, but obviously ancient. The north chancel wall is blank, its windows sealed, and the C19th east window is set within the frame of a much larger, earlier window. The Victorian restoration came late, in 1897, and the interior was much changed. It is unusual to have photos of churches before C19th remodelling, but with the restoration coming late in the century, there are at least two in existence for Fring, and they show a fine double-decker pulpit with tester on the south side (the new Victorian pulpit is on the north side) and box pews near a chancel screen, which consists of dado only. But what are not shown are the wall paintings which were uncovered much later, and which enhance the church today. They are not especially clear, but the Annunciation and St Christopher are discernible. A series of paintings runs around the angles of the south side of the chancel wall and infill an image niche. At least one window splay is painted too. All the paintings are probably C14th work. A single ?C16th inscription brass survives in front of the altar rails. Surprisingly, the C14th piscina in the sanctuary retains its original credence shelf. Next to the piscina is part of an associated sedilia set. The C13th Purbeck Marble font has characteristic arching around the octagonal bowl, but it is faint. The east window glass is modern (1984) and is beautifully crafted. There are just two tablets of note, one a plain white marble example from the mid-C18th, and the other records the sad demise of a local man in the 1st World War. In the south nave wall is a round-arched ?niche.

Views of the church from the south east, west and north east

Looking east across the nave

Chancel and sanctuary

View west from the chancel

Some of the C14th wall paintings

Inscription brass

The font

The chancel piscina

East window

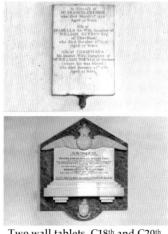

Two wall tablets, C18th and C20th

GARBOLDISHAM ST JOHN the BAPTIST   C4, TM 004 816

St John the Baptist from the south

Deep in the south of Norfolk, Garboldisham, or Garblesum to Norfolk folk, lies at the crossing of the busy A1066 and somewhat less busy B1111. There are two churches here, All Saints has been a ruin for over 300 years, but the big church of St John the Baptist is very much alive and well. A pretty footpath runs between the two buildings. There are indications that a church was here in Norman times, but the first evidence of date in the fabric are the arcades of around 1300 or possibly a little earlier. The rest of the building is C14th and C15th, and a wide-ranging restoration took place in the 1860's, overseen by G. E. Street, who rebuilt the chancel. The highlight of the exterior is the splendid C15th tower, which is a showpiece of flushwork, with the parapet, buttresses and base course all beautifully ornamented. The parapet is particularly handsome, and is distinguished by stepped battlements, religious emblems and four angel statues at the cardinal points. The west face of the tower shows clear signs of the former presence of a building, which presumably was a Galilee porch; these are distinctly rare in East Anglia. An interesting theory, which may have some validity, is that the porch was dismantled and rebuilt as the north porch. That is indeed a very grand affair, with dedications and invocations in stone to various religious figures and the donor. There is a very Victorian feel inside, but many medieval items were retained from the pre-restoration building. The possibly C13th octagonal font bowl is plain, on a C20th stem. No less than three medieval piscinas, reflecting the fact that at least two chapels were once active, can still be seen, the best of them the large twin-drain example in the chancel. The impressive nave roof is also medieval. The best of the old is the screen now guarding the entrance to the old north chapel, it may have come from All Saints. Only the dado is old and it has four panels with unusual painted figures - two female saints and St Germanus and Saint William of Norwich. The other screen across the chancel is also old, but has no painting. The best of the new is the lovely C19th and C20th stained glass from the Powell workshop, which fills most of the windows. A very fine wooden Queen Anne arms is located above the north doorway. There is a brass of 1579, complete with separate merchants mark, and a number of middle-of-the-range wall tablets. Also a 1st World War battlefield cross.

Site of Galilee porch, west face of tower   From the east   North porch

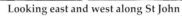

Looking east and west along St John   Battlefield cross

Chancel and screen   Chancel piscina/Queen Anne arms   The font

North aisle screen figure, St Germanus   Carlton brass (1579)   Powell glass   Powell glass/Wall tablet (1804)

Early summer at Gateley

The phrase 'off the beaten path' is arguably overused and often inappropriately applied, but there can be no argument about Gateley St Helen, it really is. Set off the tiniest of country lanes well beyond its village's boundaries, the visitor must access the church by taking a charming grassy track that runs along the side of St Helen's only neighbour, a farm, now a private dwelling. The setting is stunningly rural and the pleasant churchyard is often, in parts, left to its own devices, creating a natural oasis in the midst of the surrounding farmland. The mostly C15th building has no grand external features to set the pulse racing, but all is neat and attractive. The two early C14th doorways are the only persuasive evidence of work prior to the C15th, but the roughly coursed nave, which has ferrous conglomerate courses, almost certainly originated a lot earlier. There are no aisles and the chancel was rebuilt in the C19th, when a north vestry was also added. Look closely at the south east buttress of the tower to see two carved shields, and, behind the buttress and to the right, a mysterious arch formed partly of ferrous conglomerate blocks. At least one authority claims this is a blocked late Saxon doorway. Note also the perky double-chimney stack of the vestry. The Tudor porch has three image niches in its south wall. The nave windows are Perpendicular in style, but have curious sinuous tracery. The initial impression inside is of a sparsely filled space with little of interest, but that would be misleading. A catalogue of the features is surprisingly long, beginning with several good things near the entrance. First to catch the eye is the plain old font, its bowl monolithic and coarse, and very difficult to date. Then there is a very fine Charles I royal arms to the right of the doorway. Directly across from the arms is a painted consecration cross next to a window. Further west, two areas on the nave walls have been uncovered to reveal wall painting, decorative rather than figurative and possibly post-medieval. Further east on the nave north wall is the best of two good wall tablets, a striking heart-shaped dedication supported by putti and surrounded by clouds, of 1803. Several benches have old ends, with poppyheads and exotic arm rest animals; some have traceried backs. The C15th rood screen has an outstanding painted dado, featuring eight rarely depicted figures. The fine nave roof is C15th and the distinctive altar rails are C17th.

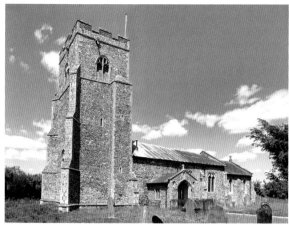

The church from the south west

The tower from the west

The buttress shields

Looking east and west along the nave

The east end and altar rails

Nave benches and bench end

Nave roof

Rood screen, northern figures

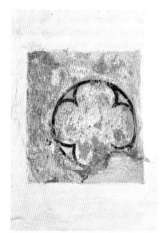

Consecration cross

The font

Sharbrook tablet (1803)

Charles I royal arms

GAYTON ST NICHOLAS

St Nicholas from the south east

Though Gayton is close to the Carstone belt, there is very little of it in St Nicholas's fabric, most of it is flint, with some pieces of 'what was to hand'. But there is much evidence of repairs and rebuilding, an interesting study in itself. Before going in, the exterior should be examined. The tower is a little odd, in that it has two sets of belfry windows, the lower have plain Y-shaped tracery of around 1300 while the upper have a Decorated design that evolved somewhat later. The buttresses extend for only a few metres from the base, and on top is an unusual dome with tall weather vane, vaulted inside. Four Evangelists symbols stand at the corners. On the east wall is an ancient roof line, steeply angled, indicating that in early days the church was thatched; it has a sanctus bell window in the apex, now external of course. Another much lower roofline can be seen inside, the present nave roof is set somewhere between the two old ones, and encloses another sanctus bell window in the east gable. The clerestory goes with the present roofline and has small, alternating, two-light and quatrefoil windows. There are two old doorways into the chancel, the blocked northern one used to open into a long-removed vestry, while the one to the south is a conventional priest's entrance. The east window is set into a much older and larger aperture, which retains its jambs. The south porch, which may be C14th, has a worn sundial of 1604. St Nicholas was restored in 1850 and that work dominates the interior. Doored pews were fitted at that time, which were usually frowned upon, but in a rural backwater, perhaps old ways still prevailed. Some old features were retained, including a very good C14th piscina and sedilia set in the chancel, enclosed within a square head. The font is an unremarkable, but pleasing, C14th example with big quatrefoils on the bowl. The nave roof is of 1850, but re-uses some old timbers. The south aisle retains an old piscina and statue plinth from a medieval chapel. Tucked up in the chancel roof apex is an odd wooden structure with a central shield, long 'legs' either side and a dove on top, probably some sort of family arms. The east window glass of 1852 is very striking, and is by George Hedgeland, who was responsible for the mighty west window in Norwich Cathedral. Wall tablets are few, but one in the chancel for the Treadway family of the 1830's is elegant. The pretty lych-gate constitutes the village war memorial.

The church from the south west and north east

The lych-gate

Interior looking east

The chancel

West from the sanctuary

North west across the church

Doored pews in the nave

Piscina, sedilia, priest's doorway

Doorway to demolished vestry

The font

South aisle piscina

In the chancel

Two scenes from the east window

Chancel roof shield

One of St Andrew's large transepts dominates the view from the south

St Andrew is a rather special church, and has a claim to possessing some of the oldest extant fabric amongst Norfolk churches. Most round towers are very old, and the debate about their true origin rumbles on, but St Andrew's has evidence of foundation in late Saxon times, based on the predominance of rough ferrous conglomerate blocks at the base and a triangular-headed window above the round-headed tower arch. Very faint traces of blocked circular windows have been reported, but are not at all obvious. The top octagonal stage of the tower is C14th. Some authorities suggest that the tower arch is also Saxon on the basis of the use of ferrous conglomerate in the construction, but there was probably later Norman alteration. It is not only the tower that has Saxon claims, lower courses of the west wall of the nave and a line of large, rough quoins at its north west corner are also of crudely hewn ferrous conglomerate. There is also some conglomerate in the chancel. Two areas of lighter, less weathered fabric around the west door and the priest's doorway into the chancel indicate where buildings once stood, a porch and a vault for the Wodehouse family, respectively. Blocked windows high in the nave south east wall and in its east wall probably once illuminated the rood. St Andrew's is also notable for its shape, it is a true cruciform church, with 'arms' of similar length. The two transepts are C14th Decorated. The interior has a great deal of interest, and reflects the lively ideas of the parishioners in the many exhibitions and projects they have organised. The 1st World War is a focus of activity, stimulated by the marvellous screen that closes off the south transept, a memorial for the fallen in the style of a medieval screen, largely painted white and complete with figures in the dado panels. The chancel was reordered by Sir Ninian Comper in 1910, and amongst the refined fixtures he introduced is a gilded reredos and a white roof with large angels and panelling with wreath ornament. A large C16th composite tomb for at least two members of the Buttes family stands in the south transept. The excellent Victorian glass is by Wailes. The font, though retooled and sparingly carved in the C19th after being found buried, is in fact medieval, as demonstrated by the filled in settings for a locking mechanism. Around it are medieval tiles found during the chancel works. The prominent west gallery houses the organ.

The tower from the south west   The chancel   From the west and the north west

Views west and east along the nave   South transept screen   Transept piscina

The chancel   Tower arch and font   Composite C16th Buttes tomb

Reredos and chancel ceiling by Sir Ninian Comper   Wailes glass

All Saints from the north as the rain comes down

The name Gresham has some resonance in Norfolk, for from here came the dynasty of the Greshams, one of whom, Sir John Gresham, founded the famous Greshams School in Holt in 1555. The setting of the village church is most pleasant and quietly rural, with a generous churchyard filled with daffodils and primroses in the Spring. The round tower of All Saints, mostly Norman and possibly earlier in the lower stage, adds distinction to what otherwise is a modest building. In the core of the west wall of the nave adjacent to the tower is the clear outline of a rectangular feature almost entirely consisting of rough ferrous conglomerate. The south end of this feature is closed off with a line of coarse ferrous conglomerate quoins, while the northern termination contains the remnants of a similarly constructed corner. These features are thought to demark the original Saxo-Norman nave. Above the outline of this early nave are indistinct indications of a possible roofline. Ferrous conglomerate can also be seen disseminated through the chancel fabric. The C15[th] south porch is grander than might be expected in such an unpretentious church, but its parvise appears disused. Inside, the plainness of the interior comes as a slight shock, for there is little ornamentation or embellishment. The reason for that is the determination of the holder of the living in the 1940's, the fiercely Puritan Lt Col. R. C. Batt, to rid the church of any feature or fitting that smacked of 'popery'. He won his battle with the incumbent of the time, and the church remains as austere as he clearly wanted it to be. That's not to say it lacks interest, there is much here to pore over and appreciate. The font has wide renown, it is a C15[th] seven sacrament example and one of the best to be seen anywhere. The vivacity of the largely undamaged panel carvings is exceptional. Nearby is the church's only surviving brass, a simple C16[th] inscription. The chancel is full of mural tablets, mostly for members of the Batt and Spurgin families. The most poignant tablet is for three sons of the aforementioned Lt Col. Batt, all killed in the 2nd World War. The oldest tablet is from 1658. The lower rood loft doorway is extant, but sealed. In the south west corner is the parvise doorway. The very good chancel glass is early Victorian and consists of formal naturalistic patterns with sacred monograms, lilies and roses. Less good is the later Victorian glass in a nave window.

Tower and nave west wall

From the south

Tower and porch

View west along the church

The chancel

West from the chancel

The font and two of its seven sacraments

Blocked rood loft entrance

Doorway to the parvise

2nd World War Batt tablet

Tablet of 1658

Inscription brass

A break in the clouds highlights St Botolph

Modern Grimston is a large village by Norfolk standards (pop. c.2000) and is distributed along and around three sides of a roughly square system of roads, but the largely C13th–C15th St Botolph lies to the south east in a lightly populated area. It is probable that the medieval village clustered closer to the church and has 'migrated' and expanded in subsequent centuries. Yet Grimston may always have been a significant settlement if the church is anything to go by, as it is large and well-appointed with an especially grand Perpendicular tower around 30m high. There are also two aisles and two short transepts, and records show that the church was embellished and extended over several centuries from a likely Saxon original. Evidence for Saxon work is a line of roughly hewn dark ferrous conglomerate quoins in the nave west wall north of the tower. The use of coarsely worked irregular blocks of ferrous conglomerate is often taken as evidence of Saxon age (the Normans preferred dressed limestone for their quoins, brought from elsewhere). By the blocked north doorway is an ancient stoup. The Early English period saw much building activity; the south doorway is a fine example. After the enticing exterior, the interior doesn't disappoint. The arcades with their stylish clustered piers attract immediate attention, but St Botolph's trump card is its woodwork. Much that is medieval remains, including the dado of the chancel screen, which has flower patterns based on those of Italian silk. To the north of the chancel arch is the lower entrance to the rood loft. On the chancel side of the screen are six excellent misericords, four with original heads beneath the seats and quaint faces at the divisions of the seats, including a monkey and a green man. Adjoining the misericords are two C14th choir stalls in fine order, these too have characterful images on the arm rests, including a mermaid, baby in chrysom robe and mythical creatures. At the west end are a few C15th benches, again with curious creatures and activities carved on the arm rests. The chancel piscina and sedilia are lovely C14th work, though heavily restored during sweeping late C19th restorations by Bodley and Garner that introduced the high-quality chancel, nave roofs and much furniture. The font is plain, with chamfered corners, and may be a survivor from the Early English church. On the south wall of the south aisle is a consecration cross.

South doorway

From the north east

Tower west face

North aisle doorway

Interior looking west and east

The chancel

Misericords and bench end figures

Screen dado

The font and tower screen

Sanctuary details

North aisle piscina

Consecration cross

HARDINGHAM ST GEORGE

C3, TG 035 051

St George seen from the sizeable churchyard

St George enjoys an enviable position on a low hill in beautiful deep Norfolk countryside. The only other building in this sequestered spot is the large picture-book country house next door, which used to be the rectory. The village of Hardingham is a significant distance away to the south. There's a crispness to St George that belies its actual age, and that is due to work carried out in the mid-C19th and probably later in the century too. However, there is much of a C13th building remaining including the unusually-sited south west tower, the chancel arch, a small north transept/chapel and parts of the generously-sized chancel. Some fittings are also C13th. The restored windows and the rest of the building are a mixture of Decorated and Perpendicular work; the east window has eye-catching network tracery. In recent times an extension was built off the nave north wall to house modern facilities, tastefully designed and constructed to match the rest of the church. Entry to St George is through a porch at the base of the tower. The deeply moulded and shafted inner doorway is probably early C13th. A low doorway inside the nave to the tower stairs has a round arch and a fine C15th door. The west end of the church has a 1st World War theme, with a striking wood and brass memorial to the fallen, with opening doors at the front, and four battlefield crosses brought back from the fighting zone after the war. Nearby is an excellent C13th tub font with traceried arching around the tub, which looks like it was once in pieces and was rebuilt. There are several superior wall memorials, the grandest, mounted to the right of the chancel arch, being for Edward Heyhoe, who died in 1788. On the other side of the chancel arch is the smaller but stylish Hogan tablet of the mid-C18th. The other tablets are all from the C19th or C20th, a good example of those is for Major W.M.M. Edwards VC (d.1912), and has his medals represented in stone below the inscription. The chancel was refitted by the Victorians, but the piscina and sedilia are a large and outstanding C13th set, the double piscina with intersecting arches and the two seats with moulded arches. In the nave south wall is another plainer piscina and next to it, a small recess for the interred heart of a long-forgotten person. The large royal arms is for George III and the plentiful, high-quality stained glass is mostly by Lavers and Westlake.

82

St George from the north east and south

Porch and south doorway

View along the nave to the chancel

From the chancel looking west

Tower stairs doorway

Double piscina and sedilia

The font

Glass by Lavers & Westlake

Heyhoe memorial

War memorial

Battlefield crosses

George III royal arms

HEACHAM ST MARY the VIRGIN

St Mary's distinctive outline is well seen from the south

Heacham enjoys a lively atmosphere, as befits a holiday village near the sea. This liveliness extends to its church, which is very active. St Mary isn't always the tidiest of places, but that is due to the good use it is put to, and it all seems to work. When people beyond the village think of Heacham, one person and one event stand out. The person is the Native American princess Pocahontas, who was brought back from America to Heacham as a bride of local lord of the manor John Rolfe in the early C17th, but sadly died soon after. She has memorials in the church. The other well-known fact about Heacham is the Heacham Declaration of 1795, when local workers and some farmers petitioned parliament to set a fair price for flour. The petition was probably the first collective action in the sense of a trade union, in Britain. The church of St Mary the Virgin is also, quite rightly, well-known. It is large, imposing and very distinctive on account of its cruciform shape, or, rather, it is a cut-down version of an early C13th cruciform church. The transepts were taken down a long time ago, but areas of walling were left to form the foundations of huge buttresses that now support the tower. A blocked-in window from the early church can be seen in the south east buttress. The chancel was also shortened because of decay, but what is left is still a powerful statement. Entry is via a once two-storey C15th porch, which shelters a superb C13th doorway, with many-moulded head and jambs with shafts bearing stiff-leaf carving in the capitals. The C15th font has a stepped base and quatrefoils on the stem, but the square bowl is plain. Many fine memorials grace the walls, several for members of the Rolfe family, and there is an impressive tomb chest of 1625 for Robert Redemayne, with black columns and a large colourful coat of arms at the top. On a pier in the organ vestry is a good medieval painting of John the Baptist and the west crossing arch has scrollwork painting. A brass of 1485 against the west wall shows an unidentified knight and John Rolfe has an inscription brass of 1594 on the north aisle wall. Six Rolfe funeral hatchments are mounted on the nave arcades. High in the apex of the chancel roof is a George III royal arms. In nave windows are eight panels of Norwich School medieval glass with excellent figures. See also the screen, a fine reading desk, brass hanging lamps, numerous first-class ledger slabs, and much more.

St Mary from the west and south east

The south doorway

View south east across the nave

West from the chancel

East from the crossing

Hanging lamp

The font

Figures from the Middle Ages

C18th? reading desk

FEAR GOD.
HONOUR THE KING.

George III royal arms

Redemayne tomb chest (1625)

Four wall tablets (1916, 1837, 1799 and 1830)

A grand church in a grand setting

The dispersed settlement of Hickling is right in the heart of The Broads tourist area, and hereabouts it can get busy in the season. But most of the action takes place by the waters of the largest of the Norfolk Broads, Hickling Broad, in the south. To the north is a much quieter area around the imposing church of St Mary, which sits serene in a large churchyard with open countryside further north. It is highly probable that a C13th or earlier church stood here, but repeated remodellings and restorations since then have left no trace of it. Especially thorough were the activities of the Victorians, who more or less gutted the interior and replaced the windows, albeit with ones of the same Decorated designs. There was much activity in Perpendicular times too, when the superb tower was made into its present form and the two-storey south porch was added. The tower west elevation is quite delightful, with a wave moulded plinth at the base. Both the doorway and large window above are elaborately finished with deep mouldings with shields running around, square heads and busy spandrel designs. The doorway spandrels feature to the north a wild (or possibly green) man in his wood, and a leafy motif to the south. A frieze of shields runs above. The window spandrels are also ornamented with shields. Above the window is a canopied niche, and above that is a square sound hole with an attractive quatrefoil design. The tower ends with large bell openings and a parapet with flushwork. The buttresses also have flushwork, as does the porch. Inside there is a feeling of space and size, but the Victorian refit left the interior with few items of significant interest. One of those is a very fine C13th tomb lid in the chancel, with floriated cross, sadly broken at the foot end. The octagonal font is good, and seems to be complete and unaltered since it was made in the C14th. The bowl design is curious, with alternation in the panels of large leaves and a double window traceried design. A rather inconsequential tomb chest in the north aisle would arouse little interest if not for the cornucopia of graffiti that adorns it, some of it from around the time of the mid-C17th civil war. The best of the few wall tablets of note is in the chancel and commemorates John Calthrop (d.1688). A pleasant corner of the north aisle is set aside for a war memorial, and has flags. The communion table is Jacobean.

St Mary from the west and north west   The two-storey porch

Looking north east across the nave   The chancel   Tomb lid

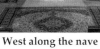

West along the nave   C16th tomb of ?Sir William Wodehouse   ...... and some of its graffiti

The font   Calthrop memorial   Gambling tablet of 1816   War memorial corner

All Saints from the south west

Hilborough All Saints is not an easy church to find despite being only a quarter of a mile or so from the A1065 road. The church is largely hidden from the road by hedges and its own avenue of trees, and the turn onto the track that leads to it is concealed until you are upon it. But the effort of finding All Saints is certainly worthwhile, for this is a church full of interest and possessing an interior where the past rapidly envelopes the visitor. The most striking feature externally is the embellished tower. The west front is very fine with its deeply moulded, shafted doorway with square head. One spandrel contains a wodewose with his club, who offers a severed head to the gentleman with a ?scimitar in the opposite spandrel. The doorway is flanked by canopied niches and flushwork arcading. Above is a frieze of shields and the coat of arms of the de Cliftons. Above that is a grand Perpendicular window. At the top is a superb lacework parapet with shields and exaggerated pinnacles. The nave next to the tower is short in length but has been raised to a good height by a bold C15th clerestory. Most of the church to this point is C14th-C15th, but the chancel is earlier. The aisles transgress onto the chancel to about half its length, and to the north a vestry fills the space to the end of the chancel. The south porch is neat and perfectly in scale, with a niche above the outer doorway and a base course with panels bearing crowned Marian monograms and symbols of St Michael. On entering, above the doorway is a great rarity, a royal arms for James I. This is quite a considerable item, and the relatively unrestored condition enhances the impact. Much of the nave seating is old, perhaps C15th, and the handsome benches have good poppyheads, openwork backs and detailed arm rests. Some later seating has low doors. The C14th font is a low, substantial example, the bowl panels adorned with quatrefoil, flower and other geometrical designs. The double piscina and sedilia set in the chancel is striking and has beautiful little springer heads; opposite is a contemporary aumbry and a cluster of tablets for members of the Caldwell family. All the roofs are medieval and despite restoration and some disfigurement, are still impressive. The angels in the nave are now headless, but the figures in the chancel are still complete. All Saints has very strong Nelson connections, Horatio's father was rector here.

The west front

From the north

Blocked south aisle window and stone coffins

View south east across the nave

Looking west

The font

Aumbry, double piscina and sedilia

Nave seating

Caldwell tablets and chancel north east

Chancel roof figure

James I royal arms

St Benedict shows off its balanced lines from the south

There are times in a Broads summer when the area around Horning can be busy, but seekers of peace and tranquillity need not fear if they choose to visit St Benedict. It lies off a narrow lane with just a few houses for company, about a mile south east of the main village. It benefits from a big, pleasant churchyard. The River Bure winds its way languidly to the sea at Great Yarmouth just a short distance away south of the church, and a pleasant path leads to St Benedict's own staithe. Externally, the church gives the impression of size, but the interior is agreeably intimate. Once there were two aisles, but the north was taken down in the early C18th, its former presence marked by the arcade entombed in the nave wall. This, along with the priest's doorway into the chancel, which has dogtooth in the hoodmould, is the oldest stonework left in the church, and is C13th. The tower is C14th and appears to taper upwards, but that is an illusion created by the diagonal buttresses stopping at the top of the second stage. Many Norfolk towers are similarly configured. The sound holes are square and have quatrefoil tracery, and standing on the tops of the pinnacles are the Four Evangelists. On the south face of the tower is an external stair turret. The interior is neat and well looked-after, but a pervasive Victorian refit left few medieval fittings and some of those remaining were restored. The north arcade can be better appreciated from the interior and is seen to have round piers. The other arcade is C14th and has octagonal piers. The font remained aloof from the C19th changes and is a battered and bruised C14th example, with arcading alternating with augmented quatrefoils on the bowl and a billet-moulded rim. The chancel has interesting choir stalls, with apparently medieval ends bearing poppyheads, arm rest figures and carvings on the panels, but there may have been some much later Victorian influence. The scenes on the ends include the jaws of hell, writhing snakes attacking a man and a cockerel within an abstract arboreal surround. A small inscription brass is mounted on a wooden plaque on the wall behind the aisle altar. There is a mutilated C14th piscina in the aisle and another better-preserved, more elaborate (and probably restored) example in the chancel, with plain drop-sill sedilia alongside. Above the piscina is what looks like a consecration cross, with fleur-de-lys processes, circular areas elsewhere may also be crosses.

The porch

St Benedict from the north east

Priest's doorway

Looking east and west along the church

Chancel and east end

View west from the chancel

Rood loft openings

Chancel piscina and sedilia

Piscina and ?consecration cross

The font

Barwick tablet

Bench end and arm rest creatures

91

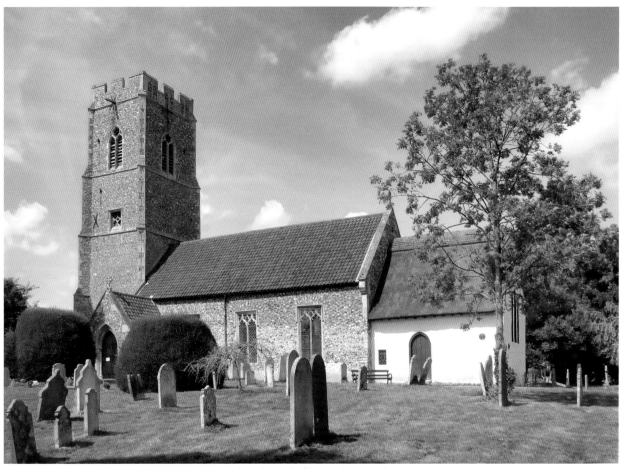

The church from the south

Horsford these days is no more than a dormitory mini-town for Norwich, an easy commute for a significant percentage of its 4000-odd population, most of whom live in the anonymous estates which comprise the main mass of north Horsford. However, the old village clusters around the church to the south and here are the last vestiges of the pre-C20th rural village. Opposite the church stands the Georgian Horsford Hall and to the north of All Saints is the palatial C19th vicarage, now one of the most desirable village residences in Norfolk. Many of the neighbouring houses are modern, but the feel is still quite rural. And All Saints is worthy of such a setting, being a distinctive building on a commanding low elevation. Most of the church is of the C14th and C15th, but the diminutive, thatched chancel is from another century, the C13th, and determinedly doesn't 'fit' with the rest. It would be very interesting to see the old church of which it was a part, which must have been much more modest than the present one, which has an imposing C15th tower and north aisle under its own gable. On the chancel gable end the date 1703 is picked out in brick, which must refer to restorations of that time. On entering All Saints a most unexpected feature attracts attention; this is a recently constructed west balcony, accessed via a chic open stairway. The balcony holds the organ. At the opposite end of the church is another world, the Early English chancel retains a sharp tang of the middle ages with three lancets in the east wall, and another in the north wall, all original. A contemporary piscina is set in the south wall. There is a large tomb recess and another less sophisticated shallow recess to the north of the altar, in which resides an ancient battlemented candle-holder. Two old, plain, black slate tablets and a low-side window with heraldic glass add to the atmosphere. The nave too has its treasures, particularly two elaborate wall memorials. The oldest is for Jane Maria Day who died in 1777; on top is a large bulbous urn and on the inscription a homily with lines from Milton's Paradise Lost and Night Thoughts by Edward Young. The other is for other members of the Day family and dates from the early C19th. The C12th font is of familiar Purbeck Marble type, with arcading on the four sides of the bowl, but is larger than many. There is a little old glass, and a touching late C19th window for three sisters who died of consumption.

All Saints from the west, north west and east

Looking west along the nave   View looking east from the balcony   Low side window

The sanctuary   The font   Candle holder in niche, chancel

Ancient and modern glass   Day family tablets of 1777 and early C19th

Recent repairs to St Lawrence's tower are clear in this view

St Lawrence lies just off a pretty, little used lane, in an enviable position. A sunny, Spring day shows the building at its best. In many ways the church is not exceptional and many similar ones occur in quiet spots all over Norfolk. However, St Lawrence has a claim to, albeit minor, fame, as for 31 years in the C19th (1848 – 1879) the incumbent here was one Rev'd James Bulwer. He was a member of a celebrated Norfolk artistic circle that included the noted painters John Sell Cotman and Frederick Sandys. Bulwer himself had broad interests both scientific and artistic, and was no mean painter in his own right, and painted pictures of Hunworth church and other Norfolk churches such as Morston and Saxthorpe. He commissioned others from artists of the Norwich School and part of his large collection of paintings and drawings, housed in Norwich Castle Museum, is of more than regional importance. He also oversaw important restorations and the rebuilding of the chancel at Hunworth around 1850, and is buried in the churchyard. He would recognise much of his work in the present St Lawrence, as very little has changed since his time. The nave has traces of Norman quoins which delimit the original small church, and there is rough ferrous conglomerate in the fabric. A double-splayed window in the nave south wall is variously dated as late Saxon or early Norman. It has been suggested that the tower is also an early, perhaps C12th structure, but little or nothing remains to confirm that, and the appearance today is that of a C15th structure; the tower was recently extensively repaired. There are no aisles, but a C15th transept built off the nave south wall originally housed a chapel. The interior is plain and unadorned, and rather stark as a result. There is almost nothing on the walls, and a marked lack of flair in the furnishings, which, nevertheless, are of good quality. The chapel is now converted for bench seating but the original piscina remains, partly hidden by a mass of electricity boxes. The C14th or C15th octagonal font is quite plain and unremarkable. A couple of formidable ledger slabs provide a focus of interest; both are for members of the locally important Britiffe family. They are for father and son, both Edmund, and their wives, and are from the early and late C18th respectively. Some of the bench poppyheads bear plain shields. A niche in a north nave window arris holds a modern statue of St Lawrence.

St Lawrence from the east and west

The porch

Double-splay window

Looking east

.... and west

The font

The sanctuary

Transept piscina

Britiffe ledger slab

The pulpit

Poppyhead

Great War plaque

Many have passed this way ...

INGWORTH ST LAWRENCE

St Lawrence on its ancient mound

St Lawrence is a super little church, packed with character and interest. The vicissitudes it has clearly suffered over the centuries simply add more distinction, and the gloriously idiosyncratic interior with its many antique features is a pleasure to explore. The setting in a sub-circular churchyard on a mound may well be very ancient, and St Lawrence looks a picture in it. The building may have begun life in the C11th as a simple one cell construction, the rough, dark ferrous conglomerate quoins of which can still be seen at the north west corner. Coarsely dressed ferrous conglomerate blocks elsewhere in the fabric support early foundation. The round tower may be contemporary, as the semi-circular arch inside is of primitive build suggestive of pre-Norman work. The tower collapsed in 1822 and the stump was later converted very successfully into a thatched vestry. The chancel dates from the C13th, and major works took place in the C15th when the nave south wall was moved outwards and the charming two-storey porch added. The latter has a crow-step brick gable, added in the C16th. Box pews were installed in the C18th, and thereafter the church was fortunate not to be spoilt by Victorian remodelling, leaving the splendidly atmospheric interior that characterises St Lawrence today. The compact space is pleasantly crowded with fittings, and the first one to draw attention on entering via the south doorway is the unusual balcony on the north nave wall. This houses the organ. Below it a range of box pews, one with carved back, extends east to the pulpit. Mounted on a finial on the easternmost pew is a rare hourglass stand, seemingly still in working order. Benches on the south side appear to be cut down and modified box pews, or are perhaps contemporary open versions. The pulpit is the much reduced result of cutting-down an earlier C17th triple-decker. Near it, the screen is medieval in the lower sections with pretty carving, but has no paintings or figures. The C14th font has a plain bowl, but it has been suggested that it may once have borne carvings of the seven sacraments. Next to it set into the brick floor is an early stone coffin lid. The altar rails are a delightful C18th set with barley-twist balusters. On the nave west wall is a rare and opulent royal arms for William III. There is an excellent panel of ?C17th continental glass in the east window and elsewhere a small Saint's head of medieval English origin.

The truncated tower

From the south east

Porch and west end

Looking east along the nave

The sanctuary

West end, tower arch and font

Screen, pulpit, rood loft doorways

Carved bench back

Coffin lid

Sanctuary memorial

C17th continental and C14th English glass

Hourglass near pulpit

William III royal arms

St Mary from the south east

Once a Norman church stood on this site, but only the south doorway remains from that building. This has a classic Romanesque embellished design with fluted capitals and dogtooth ornament on the imposts and arch mouldings. All the rest of the Norman church was swept away by remodellings in the early C14th (chancel, north aisle), and, especially, in the C15th and early C16th centuries. The tower and much of the rest of the church is from that interval. Later, a wide-ranging makeover was undertaken in the C19th. After all those building campaigns the church we see today is impressive, although the tower was surely never finished. The windows are many and large, and there is a low-side window in the south chancel wall which was later extended upwards. The clerestory is present on both sides of the nave, despite there being only a north aisle. All those windows admit generous light into the interior, creating an airy and calm space. There are a great many features and fittings to beguile the visitor, many surviving from the medieval church. The C14th font itself is unexceptional, but it has a most impressive tall cover, also C14th and consisting of buttresses forming a tapering tower with an odd, later, inverted flaring finial on the top. One rare royal arms would be notable, but St Mary has two. The oldest is for Elizabeth I and was made to fit the chancel arch, it now resides in the north aisle. It bears a fabulous spotted red dragon. The other arms is for Charles I and this is mounted above the north doorway. Both arms are on slatted board. In the south nave wall is an old piscina, a crude depression next to it may be a single sedile. The chancel piscina is also old, but plainer; next to it the sedilia are contained within a wide niche. On the other side of the chancel stand the remains of a tomb chest from around 1500, with its extremities damaged. Above it is a very good tryptych with a crucifixion theme, and above that one of the many excellent wall tablets that adorn the church. A few medieval benches still survive, but most are in poor condition. There is a plain pillar poor box. Two fragments of a brass of c.1500 are mounted on the south nave wall, depicting children. Next to them are two small plinths for statues, two more are set on the chancel arch pillars. Three C19th and C20th windows have fine glass by Heaton, Butler and Bayne. The ornate stone pulpit is Victorian. By the south doorway is a medieval holy water stoup.

St Mary from the west and north west

Norman south doorway

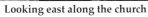

Looking east along the church

View west from the sanctuary

Font and cover

Nave piscina and sedile

Chancel piscina and sedilia in niche

Glass by Heaton, Butler & Bayne 1928

Truncated tomb and tryptych

Groome tablet, mid-C18th

Elizabeth I and Charles I royal arms

99

KIMBERLEY ST PETER

The evening sun illuminates St Peter

Sometimes, particularly in winter, St Peter can be glimpsed through the trees from the B1108 road, and seems to be inviting a visit. The invitation should be accepted, for this is a church with more than passing interest. For much of its existence St Peter was a 'Hall church', under the sponsorship of the Wodehows/Wodehouses/Woodhouses of Kimberley Hall. Many of their memorials can be seen in the church. Externally St Peter is unexceptional, there are no aisles, although at one time it may have had a chapel off the nave north wall. Most of the windows are replacements and the top part of the tower was rebuilt in 1631, a date recorded in brick on its walls. The modest porch is C14th, the rest of the building is C14th-C15th. There were sweeping renovations and refittings in 1875 and 1904, most of the furnishings and the hammerbeam nave roof date from those campaigns. St Peter boasts a collection of exceptional C14th-C16th stained glass, housed in the east and other chancel windows. Little if any of this is indigenous to the church, although some is English. The rest is mostly German, and its origin goes back to those troubled times of revolution and war in Europe in the C18th-C19th when many religious establishments were ransacked and their treasures dispersed. Alert entrepreneurs in Britain in the C19th were quick to see a business opportunity and some of these treasures, especially old window glass and woodwork, found their way to Britain. The foreign glass at Kimberley was acquired and sold on by the well-known figure of J. C. Hampp, as was the even finer collection at nearby Hingham. The best English pieces are a figure of St Margaret of Antioch (c.1375), St Catherine with her wheel, St John the Baptist and angels; superb German glass from Cologne Cathedral also includes angels. Sadly some panels have become blackened and detail obscured. Elsewhere in St Peter is a good wall memorial for Elizabeth Strutt (d.1651), a brass of c.1530 for John and Constance Wodehows (John died earlier in 1465) and another Wodehows brass which is inscription only. The elaborate royal arms for James I is rare enough, but the motto *Beati Pacifici* is rarer still. The entrance to the rood loft has been converted to a niche, while across the nave from it is another niche. There are several fine ledger slabs for members of the Woodhouse family. The font is C14th, with shields, and the trefoil-headed chancel piscina is also C14th.

St Peter from the south west, north west and west

West from the sanctuary   East from the font   James I royal arms

An angel from Cologne   St Margaret of Antioch   An English angel   The moon and the sun

C19th glass by Clayton & Bell   Sir T Wodehouse (d.1658) ledger   For Elizabeth Strutt (d.1651)   Wodehows brass, fabricated c.1530

KIRBY BEDON ST ANDREW

A beautiful day at St Andrew

St Andrew was thoroughly restored and largely rebuilt in 1876, and in 1884 the tower and porch were renewed, but even such drastic modifications failed to extinguish the charm both of the church and the setting. The interior also saw extensive refitting but, again, the attractiveness and appeal were retained. Many fine features add to the pleasing ambience. And today, dedicated stewardship ensures that this state of affairs continues, making St Andrew a worthy objective for a visit. Before entering, a walk around the churchyard of any church is always recommended, and here it is especially rewarding, for in a sylvan setting to the north west of the church is the Harvey mausoleum of 1868, a miniature gothick church in its own right. A sad story pertains to the mausoleum, as inside are the remains of Sir R. J. Harvey, who presided over the Crown Bank in Norwich during its collapse in 1870, partly as a result of his own unwise speculations. When the facts were known, Sir Robert shot himself. A surprise awaits inside the porch, for here is a Norman doorway, plainer than some, but still in good order. Perhaps more important than the doorway is the door itself, which is either Norman or Early English. Its intricate and fascinating ironwork may be as early as C12th. A holy water stoup is set alongside the doorway, and there is another in a corresponding position inside. The C15th font standing close to the inner doorway has arcading on the bowl panels and similar ornament on the stem, also an odd, but nicely-worked, Jacobean cover, resembling a flat hat. A glance along the church reveals several wall tablets and memorials, particularly in the chancel. Many of these are of more than passing interest, either for their elaborate designs or their inscriptions. The oldest is a prie-dieu example of 1600 and is for Robert and Anne Sheppard. Nearby on the chancel east wall is an impressive tablet for Jane Brooke of 1786. Complementing the wall memorials are numerous large ledger slabs set into the floors, and four brasses. Two are inscription only, one of which is partly concealed beneath the sturdy C18th pulpit. One other is a shroud brass of 1505 in the nave, whilst in the chancel is a mid-C15th heart brass with scrolls. The handsome communion rails are late C17th. The crude, simple piscina is associated with drop-sill sedilia. Some old glass is collected in nave windows, this includes a C14th angel busily engraving.

St Andrew from the south west

The Harvey mausoleum

South doorway and stoup

View across the nave

Chancel and sanctuary

Looking west from the altar

C18th pulpit

Font and cover

Dussyng shroud brass (1505)

Heart brass (mid-C15th)

Jane Brooke tablet (1786)

Sheppard memorial (1600)

Angel engraver

A corner of the sanctuary

LITTLE DUNHAM ST MARGARET

B/C2, TF 864 130

St Margaret from the south west

This delightfully set church is often overlooked in favour of its more celebrated sister church nearby at Great Dunham, which has significant Saxon elements, but after viewing that building it is well worth coming here. First of all, the setting is tranquil and reflective, and then the building itself has much to offer. The plan is tower, short nave with north aisle, chancel and south porch. A north chancel arcade, now filled-in, once opened into a chapel. The fabric has an attractive patina of age, although the custodians of the church might not agree as they contemplate the leaning walls of the chancel. The building contains work from the C13th to the C15th and the three major medieval periods of ecclesiastical architecture are represented; the nave and chancel are Early English, the north aisle is Decorated and the tower Perpendicular. The windows largely conform with these assignments, but later replacements are also present and there is some Victorian influence, although that is more noticeable inside. The excellent south doorway is of typical Early English form, while the west doorway into the tower is as characteristically Perpendicular, as is its companion window above. The nobly decaying interior is a pleasure to experience and explore. The C13th arcade to the aisle, with its lovely clustered piers, continues on as an arcade to a long-demolished north chapel. On the west respond of the chancel section of the arcade is a singular head stop, variously described as a 'demon', 'bull', 'man with horns' or 'green man'. The head is set in foliage, but the face is so damaged as to render accurate assignment difficult. Notwithstanding, the effect on the onlooker can be quite disturbing. Also on the chancel arcade arches are remnants of medieval decorative painting, and on one pier a consecration cross survives. The C14th font is handsome if rather bland, but is enlivened by a series of distinctive heads beneath the bowl, with glum expressions. Charles Nelson (d.1841), a member of the Nelson clan, is commemorated on a brass floor plate and a wall tablet. Two other fine C18th wall tablets are mounted on the south wall, one for Emelia Parry (d.1791), the other for Thomas Rogers (d.1758). Near the pulpit is a rather distressed piscina, but a better example is the angle piscina in the chancel, next to which are drop-sill sedilia, with arm rest. Next to the south doorway is an old holy water stoup.

Views from the west and north west   The south doorway

The interior looking east and west   A corner of the sanctuary

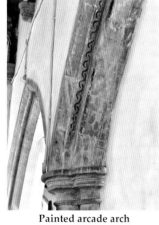

Painted arcade arch   Curious head stop   The font   Font heads

Battered nave piscina   Consecration cross   Charles Nelson (d.1841)   For Thomas Rogers (d.1758)

LITTLE ELLINGHAM ST PETER

C3, TM 005 992

St Peter from the south east

Many churches have suffered the ravages of fire, which can completely or partly destroy a building. St Peter was one of the unlucky ones, and lost almost everything in a fire in 1867, only the C14th tower and parts of some walls, particularly those of the chancel, were spared. But like so many others, a concerted effort was made to rebuild St Peter in 1869, and, almost as importantly, to salvage what little remained and incorporate it in the new nave and chancel. The contractors were T.H. and F. Healey. Also, unusually, some of the pre-fire features were reproduced and set in their old positions. It seems that the tower always stood off to the south west, and incorporated the main entrance at its base, and this adds distinction to what otherwise would be an unremarkable, mostly Victorian church. Above the outer doorway is a figure niche and the inner doorway appears to be original C14th work. In the later C19th a vestry was tucked in to the west of the tower, adding another singular feature to St Peter. As would be expected the interior is almost all post-fire, but a few items from the old church were retrieved. The simple piscina in the south east nave wall is clearly medieval, and up in the sanctuary is an old stone shelf beneath which are three battered corbel heads. Is this an amalgamation of disparate parts, or part of an original structure? In the head of a chancel window there is a small collection of medieval glass fragments, mostly indistinct and non-figurative, but they include a splendid head of an angel, very small and typical of the Norwich School of stained glass, with, to its left, an even smaller head. The Victorian stained glass is of excellent quality, but the artists could not be identified. The nave north east window has the look of the Kempe workshop, but lacks the usual wheatsheaf mark, and the east window resembles the work of William Wailes. Much later than the medieval survivals, but still pre-fire, is a classic High Victorian wall tablet and in the floor near the sanctuary is a large late C18th floor slab for Thomas and Mary Bond. The Victorian font is an eye-catching example with a shiny bowl made of a dark, igneous stone, on contrasting pillars. The bowl bears Trinity symbols. Oddly, a large, empty niche on the north nave wall with a smaller one alongside were remade in 1869 after the originals were destroyed.

106

Tower and vestry

Views from the north and west

Interior looking east

The east end

Interior looking west

The font

Nave piscina

Stone shelf in the sanctuary

Bond ledger slab

Mid-19th wall tablet

Nave north west window

East window

Norwich School angel

The church from the south west

Little Melton is a scattered parish situated a few miles west of Norwich. The proximity of the city exerts little or no effect on the village, and it retains a strong rural atmosphere. St Mary stands alone some way west of the main settlement of today, but archaeological finds suggest that the early medieval village probably clustered around the church. These discoveries are from the late Saxon period and perhaps indicate that a Saxon building stood here. However, the present building mostly dates from around 1300 (restored 1896) and exudes a mellow antiquity and harmony, as well as possessing a great deal of interest for the historian. There are several lancet and Y-shaped windows characteristic of the early C14th, the long lancet in the chancel south wall also functioned as a low-side window. From the south the aisled building is beautifully balanced, but to the north coming off the north aisle is an extension of 2009. Its modern lines and materials are not in sympathy with the pre-existing architecture, and, though the extension offers a much-needed addition to the church's facilities, it is aesthetically jarring. Inside, there is a lot to see and absorb. The narrow aisles indicate that they were built not long after the main body of the church. In the southern one near the entrance stands a substantial C13th Purbeck Marble font, very typical, and of a kind often found in Norfolk, with arcading around the octagonal bowl. The grand old cover is also noteworthy. The handsome chancel screen is C15th and very well preserved, with red and green painted panels and lovely tracery above. The pulpit and some other fittings were constructed from parts of a medieval screen that once partitioned off the north chapel. The chancel has some fine wall memorials, including two large and showy examples from 1656 and the early C18th, also several smaller copper tablets for members of the Scottowe family. The C14th double piscina and sedilia set is most attractive. Another super piscina is set in the north arcade east respond. Several medieval paintings have been revealed on the walls by removing generations of whitewash and paint, the best depict the evils of gossip, and the Annunciation on the east wall. A good set of rood stairs is entombed high up in the north aisle wall. An inscription brass of 1604 for Dorothy and Robert Angwish is set in the floor near the pulpit, with the Angwish arms beneath. Near the entrance is a plain holy water stoup.

Tower and porch

Looking from the south east and north east

Interior looking east

The east end

Interior looking west

The chancel screen

Double piscina and sedilia

Font and cover

Scottowe memorial (1656)

Piscina in north arcade

Rood loft steps

Angwish plate (top), Evils of Gossip (bottom)

War memorial and St Andrew and St Peter

St Andrew stands some way west of its parent village, with only Longham Hall for company. Visitors expecting a classic English grouping of church and hall in a sylvan setting might be a little disappointed to see that Longham Hall is more a grand farmhouse than a hall, and is associated with considerable commercial activity. It was built around 1840. Since the removal of most of the gravestones north of the long approach path, St Andrew can seem a mite austere on a rainy day, but the church looks well when the sun shines. Victorian restorers took a special interest in St Andrew and doubtless a lot of its medieval character was eradicated during extensive works that included rebuilding the chancel, replacing or restoring most of the windows, re-roofing and a thorough refurnishing inside. Most of the old work and the tower are C14th and C15th. The steepness of the nave roof suggests that it was once thatched. There are no aisles, but there is a Perpendicular south porch with a composite outer arch of ill-matched parts, and maybe other 'borrowed' details. However, there is no doubting that it has character. To the north is a Victorian vestry. The tower, due to the configuration of the buttresses and a short top stage, looks squat and somewhat rectangular. Its earlier top stage was removed in 1788 and was replaced with a shorter one in the late C19th. Though well-maintained, the interior is short on interesting features, and the 'new' chancel is bland, with the exception of almost the only wall tablet in the church, a partly old communion table and a nicely carved reredos. Said tablet is for a parish worthy, John Hastings, who died in 1869. Both rood loft doorways and stairs survive and are excellent examples. A small slit is cut into the close-by window embrasure to light the stairway. The nave south east and north east windows have slots which accommodated the long-removed rood beam, but the C15th chancel screen is too high for a beam above it to have fitted into the slots, so the screen probably came from elsewhere. It has attractive Perpendicular tracery at the top, and the merest hint of painted figures on the dado, which itself has fine tracery in the panel heads. A curiosity is the presence of the drain plate of an old piscina built into the apex of the nave south east window. Next to the chancel arch is a plain niche. The modest font may be C15th, with later, probably C19th, restoration.

Fast falls the eventide

The porch

The south doorway

Original closing ring

Interior looking east

Chancel screen

Screen panels

Screen tracery

Chancel and sanctuary

West end and tower arch

The font

Rood loft doorways, niche

Rood beam support

Piscina base reset in a window

Hastings tablet (1869)

MARSHAM ALL SAINTS

All Saints from the south west

All Saints is a familiar sight for road users on the main A140 Norwich to Cromer road, which passes nearby, although it is usually just a glimpse through the trees. Very few ever stop however, which is a shame as this is a church worthy of a detour. It has some interesting historical connections too, as one of its incumbents in the late C17th, the Rev'd Samuel Oates, was father to the 'Popish Plotter' Titus Oates, who invented a tale about Catholics scheming to assassinate Charles II. His spurious 'evidence' led to many executions, but he was found out, and dealt with very violently, but not executed. Another rector was Henry Cavell, the uncle of the first world war heroine Edith Cavell. Externally the mainly C14th and C15th church (the south doorway is C13th) holds no great surprises, it is aisled with a good clerestory and the tower has a plain parapet. But inside there are some excellent things. A striking C15th, octagonal, well-preserved, seven sacrament font greets the visitor as they enter. The eighth bowl panel depicts the Day of Judgement. Most heads have been hammered off, but all the sacraments are easily discernible, and the rest of the font, with Evangelists around the stem, is also very impressive. Above the font is a modern organ gallery, and on the front of that is mounted a rare royal arms for James I, in very good order despite some fading of the colours. Higher still is a C15th nave roof of hammerbeam type, with wooden angels on the hammers, the whole in excellent order. The cross beams are later, inserted to hold up a listing south aisle. The excellent woodwork doesn't end with the nave roof, across the chancel arch is one of Norfolk's best rood screens, dated by donations to 1503-09. The arch being wide, there is room for 16 panels on the dado, two blank. The rest bear representations of Saints, who have stood the test of time well, despite suffering some defacement in unsettled times. Above, the tracery is delicate and elegant. Another plus for All Saints is the stained glass. A little medieval glass is set into aisle windows, including the ?unique depictions in East Anglia of a unicorn and an elephant, and also larger figures of King David and Judas Maccabeus. The glass in the chancel, from around the turn of the C20th, is excellent. The east window may be by Powell and Son, and a south window came from the Kempe workshop. Old poppyheads adorn several benches.

Two views of All Saints from the west and the south east • South doorway

Interior looking east and west • Nave roof

Roof angels large and small • The font • James 1st royal arms • Glass by Kempe

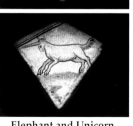

Elephant and Unicorn • The rood screen and some of its dado figures

The oddly positioned north west tower is well seen from the north east

Mileham is steeped in history, with evidence of long occupation. It is thought the Romans had a settlement here, and many of their artefacts have been unearthed. There are also the remains of a Norman castle complex built around 1100, a deserted medieval village site and a super church with many unusual features. The romantic castle site is best seen from the air from where the circular plan, twin baileys, motte, moat and rectangular enclosure across the road from the main castle are very clear. The church probably dates from around the heyday of the castle and it seems likely there were strong links between them. The Norman evidence in St John has largely been lost over the centuries (but see the chancel doorway) and most of the building dates from the C13th–C15th. The plan is odd, with the C14th tower sited off the north west corner of the church, let slightly into the C13th north aisle to allow access from it. There are two aisles and a clerestory. The interior is full of remarkable features and fittings. Pride of place must go to the medieval glass, especially the west window which incredibly retains a great deal of original glass in situ, some of the best in Norfolk, plus some later medieval work. The south aisle east window also has some splendid C14th pieces. At the other end of the time scale, the chancel east window contains a striking modern representation of the baptism of Christ from the C21st. Both aisles have fine C15th roofs with attractive tracery in the spandrels, and both also have piscinas to indicate their former use as chapels. The C14th font is set on a high pedestal and has quatrefoils on the bowl, and the two damaged niches in the east wall are probably contemporary with it. Also C14th are two well-preserved tomb lids with foliate crosses, set next to doorways. The pulpit is a graceful C15th example perched on a single slender pillar. The poor box from 1639 is a typical example from a time when such things were produced in large numbers. The Crowe family brass (c.1526) in the south aisle is excellent and almost complete. Many fine memorials grace the walls and floors, ranging from the elaborate Barnwell tablets in the chancel to a number of rustic tablets of more than passing interest. The ledger slabs before the altar record intimate details of family tragedies, including those of the Pepys family. The Victorian nave benches are a neat set, with doors. There are rood stairs in the north aisle.

The top of the tower

St John seen from the south east

Blocked chancel doorway

The interior looking north east and west

Crowe brass (c.1526)

West window and examples of the superb medieval stained glass

The pulpit

Poor box (1639)

The font

Medieval stone tomb covers

Barnwell tablets (early C19th & late C18th)

Fine ledger slabs

115

The late C18th Butter tomb dominates the foreground in this view of All Saints

Sometime around 1855 the Rev'd James Bulwer, the vicar of Hunworth, came to Morston on one of his frequent painting expeditions and painted two lovely watercolours of All Saints. The viewpoints he used are much the same today and although the water he painted in his view from the east has gone, Morston church is still a grand objective for an expedition of any sort, and painters still visit the spot. It is said that Sir Alfred Munnings was painting the church when war was declared on Sept 3rd 1939. The building has ancient roots and the tower would seem to be a largely C12th structure, on the evidence of the narrow round-headed slit windows to the south and west. In the mid-C18th a large portion of the upper tower collapsed, and was repaired in brick. The collapse is given as the explanation for the unusual configuration of the nave parapet, which has lost some of its battlements, but the reason for the change from ?early C13th quatrefoil windows to two finished in the C15th-C16th Tudor style in the south clerestory is more obscure. The body of the aisled building is C13th-C14th with most windows being in the Decorated style, but the east window must be a C19th replacement, as Bulwer's painting shows a Perpendicular window here. All Saints underwent quite heavy Victorian restoration so perhaps other windows are also replacements. The two porches are C15th or C16th. There is lots to investigate inside. The C15th font stands on a high plinth of a Maltese Cross pattern, and has the Evangelists and their symbols on the bowl. The dado of a late C15th rood screen closes off the chancel and is in excellent order, with paintings of the Four Evangelists and the Four Latin Doctors in the panels, with exquisitely carved (but largely beheaded) angels and other entities in the spandrels. The screen was restored in 1988. To the right of the screen is a pretty wall tablet of 1615 with a carved alabaster surround. Many of the old floor slabs tell compelling tales. Above the chancel arch is a large, dark and almost illegible wooden royal arms of 1823 with a Decalogue, Creed and Lord's Prayer board below. In the chancel is a C13th angle piscina and plain sedilia, C17th altar rails and communion table, with beneath the latter a fine brass of 1596, unfortunately difficult to see. On the responds of the arcades are some droll old head stops, not a smile in sight! There is a single small panel of medieval canopy glass in the west window.

All Saints from the north west, south east and west

The interior looking east and west   Chancel and sanctuary   The font

George IV royal arms, Decalogue, Creed, Lord's Prayer   The C15th screen dado

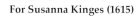

For Susanna Kinges (1615)   For Robart Powdich (1647)   Head stops   Angle piscina

117

A bitter winter's day sees St Andrew under light snow

St Andrew was largely rebuilt in 1863, only the tower and north transept were retained from the old church, which was in a poor state, apparently. Because of this the building receives little attention and its excellent Victorian features are overlooked. But there is no doubt that the architect of the rebuilding, the little known D. Male (even his christian name is elusive), did a good and conscientious job. From the evidence of the transept, the old church was mostly Perpendicular in style, but Male fitted the church mostly with curvilinear Decorated windows. These are most effective and add style, but there is no doubt that the star window is the transept north with its grand Perpendicular design. In the nave north wall windows, Male reflected the design of what are presumably the original Perpendicular belfry windows. As might be expected the interior has a complete Victorian furnishing scheme, and very little of the earlier church was retained, but it was a project of high aspiration and is an excellent tutorial into the minds and methods of the Victorian Gothic revivalists. What's more, the interior is little changed from 1863. Almost the only things to survive from the earlier building in the body of the church are a couple of wall memorials in the chancel, the Holman tablet from the early C19[th] and the Custance memorial from just before the rebuilding. Also a choice grave slab from c.1320 in the aisle, which has consecration crosses and may later have served as an altar. High on the internal tower wall is a medieval sanctus bell window, almost hidden by the fine C19[th] nave roof. The chancel roof is also a work of outstanding quality. Indeed, many of the finest Victorian features are found in the chancel, for example, the reredos set into the wall behind the altar is an admirable example of mosaic work in glass by the famous Italian designer Salviati. The sympathetic lighting installed in the church shows off the designer's superb touch very well. The plentiful window glass is also first class. Most of it is by the firm of O'Connor, but the west window, now a little difficult to appreciate due to the modern glass screen infilling the tower arch, is by Powell and Son, using templates designed by Henry Holiday. Both the pulpit and the font are of superior workmanship, the former enhanced by brass roundels and excellent carvings while the latter has a sturdy, almost classical appearance. A grand chest of 1864 stands near the south doorway.

Tower and porch

St Andrew from the north west

The north transept

Interior looking east

Chancel and sanctuary

View west from the sanctuary

Nave roof and sanctus bell window

East window glass, angels and St Michael

Wall memorials

Grave slab c.1320

The pulpit

The font

Chancel roof angel

119

OLD BUCKENHAM ALL SAINTS

The church from the south west

All Saints is a striking and unusual church, and delightful too, with a very rare octagonal tower. Many of the C11th–C13th round-towered churches of East Anglia have later octagonal upper stages, but only half a dozen or so are octagonal for their full length. It is debatable how many of these were originally built as such, it seems that some are merely later shells around a round tower. This view is reinforced by the fact that the interior of the Old Buckenham tower is round, as are others in the octagonal series. But one thing is certain, and that is that All Saints is of ancient foundation, its dimensions, low barn-like structure and rough ferrous conglomerate in the fabric are characteristic of Norman and earlier churches. The aisle was added a century or so later, so the north doorway of typical round-headed Norman form was clearly relocated from elsewhere. Another feature of the north side are the aisle buttresses, on which are mounted sacred monograms carved in stone. The C14th porch has just been enlivened by the appearance of a grotesque face, carved on a Norman voussoir stone. This faced inwards until turned around recently. Inside there are some lovely features to admire. There is superb stained glass of both medieval and Victorian origin. The medieval glass is found in two Perpendicular south windows in the nave, and fills the tracery at the tops. Below is Victorian glass, in one window of excellent quality (by C. E. Kempe), in the other rather less so. The C15th glass is fragmentary and from mixed sources, but some imaginative reconstruction work has introduced a coherent structure. Featured most prominently are angels of typical Norwich School type, but there are also a few Saints and a series of shields of important local families. Very recently the old glass was taken out and restored, and now can be seen in all its glory. The choir stalls of 1931 incorporate old bench ends with poppyheads and prophets and apostles on the arm-rests, which form a fine show in the chancel. The C15th font has shields and quatrefoils on the bowl, with sour faces beneath. The faded royal arms are for George III. A partly medieval restored screen, once across the chancel, closes off a vestry at the west end. The old bier is dated 1655. An oddity is a chunky wall tablet in the chancel which pertains to be C17th, but in fact dates only from 1922. A number of old stone heads adorn the walls as head stops or are freestanding.

All Saints from the west and the north

Norman north doorway & monogram

Looking east along the nave

The church from the sanctuary

The east end

Examples of the medieval glass in the nave south windows

Kempe glass

Choir stalls and figures

The font

George III royal arms

St Margaret from the south churchyard

The name Paston has become immortalised thanks to the publication of letters and documents of the Paston family, who lived in this small north Norfolk village from the late C14th to the mid-C18th, and took their name from it. The family began as peasants and by shrewd manoeuvering ended up as minor aristocracy, and their doings between 1422 and 1509, recorded in remarkable letters, were later published to great acclaim. Paston is also well-known for its Great Barn of 1581, built by the Pastons, one of the largest and best of its kind. A long term restoration is nearing completion. St Margaret has no aisles, but the nave is very wide, creating a barn-like feel within. Most of the church dates from the C14th and there are some agreeable Decorated windows; however, most if not all windows are C19th replacements, probably following the design of the medieval antecedents. The tower buttresses only rise to halfway. There is much of interest inside. The chancel is filled with Paston tombs, monuments and a brass of c.1575 for Erasmus Darwin, unfortunately missing his wife's brass. The simpler and earlier chest tombs came from Bromholm Priory when it was decommissioned at the Reformation, and in one case at least, were inserted with little regard for existing features. The tomb in question was rudely installed in the sedilia recess. The chest tombs and everything else are overshadowed by two huge, contrasting C17th memorials. The tomb of Katherine Paston (1629) is exuberant but rather overbearing, while its neighbour for Edward Paston (1632) is almost clinically Classical. Both are by Nicholas Stone. From an earlier age, the chancel angle piscina has five orders of mouldings in its trefoil head and a pillar drain. St Margaret has two good medieval wall paintings, and traces of several more. The clearest two depict St Christopher, opposite the south door as is usual, and the morality tale of the Three Living and the Three Dead. The screen has been remade but retains some C15th elements. The C14th octagonal font is raised on two steps and has Decorated tracery on the bowl panels. The C19th and C20th glass is distinctive and of high quality. A reading desk and several poppyheads are old, the former has elegant tracery and the latter include Paston heraldry and an impudent face. Above the tower arch is a fine arms of William IV. The unusual rotund, ornate altar rails came from a private house and may be C17th or C18th.

Views from the north and the south west

Paston arms poppyhead

The interior looking east

The chancel and sanctuary

Mack memorial window (1917)

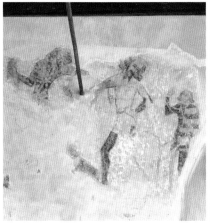   

Part of the '3 living and the 3 dead'

St Christopher

William IV royal arms

Katherine Paston monument

The font

Chancel piscina & sedilia, with inserted tomb

Erasmus Darwin c.1575

Reading desk

123

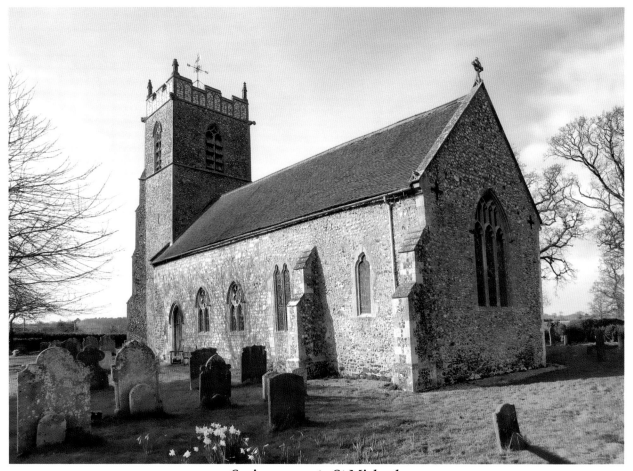

Spring comes to St Michael

The contrast between exterior and interior of the likeable church of St Michael is very marked. Externally there are features indicating great age, whilst inside the look and feel is of a classic Victorian/early C20th church. The external features are concentrated to the west of the main south door and consist of areas of walling with herringbone coursing and much use of ferrous conglomerate. Also, there are two lines of quoins indicating different periods of early building, one of them constructed with ferrous conglomerate. Another line of quoins to the east demarcates the eastern end of the early nave. All these features are consistent with a C12th date for the construction of the nave, and thus probably for the original church. Also on the south side there used to be an aisle, taken down in the C18th, but the Perpendicular arcade survives entombed in the wall. It is well seen inside the church. The battlemented tower parapet has some smart flushwork panelling and is crowned by pinnacles. The base of the tower also has flushwork. There is no porch to the south, but a neat ?Victorian one exists to the north, now disused as an entrance. The interior is well-ordered, and was almost entirely refitted in 1873, but some interesting older features are preserved. A few panels of fine old glass of both English and continental origin has been gathered in the east and south windows. This was only installed in 1952 and originated from Catton Hall, near Norwich. The east window glass includes two excellent, almost complete C15th figures of the Norwich School, one certainly St Agnes, the other a saint, sometimes identified as St John. Two other panels have good figures, supported by a jumble of fragments, and these are St Bartholomew with his symbol, a flaying knife, and another who is a prior or bishop, with crozier. There are also three quatrefoils with heads, an Agnus Dei and a composite angel, plus fragments in all. In the south windows is C17th continental glass, which depicts a rather remarkable ascending angel and two roundels showing St Michael killing the dragon. Elsewhere inside is a plain C14th font on a much later stem and base, a section of an Easter sepulchre with garish colouring, a rustic but endearing wall tablet of 1742 and a very rare royal arms for George VI. This latter has the words, 'In memory of H. M. King George VI', so may have been erected after his death. The chancel piscina is old, but much restored.

St Michael from the west and north west   Ancient walling

Interior looking east   The east end   The nave looking west

Part of an Easter sepulchre   Font and cover   Fleming tablet (1742)   Roof angel

Continental and English glass   St Michael dispatches the dragon   George VI royal arms

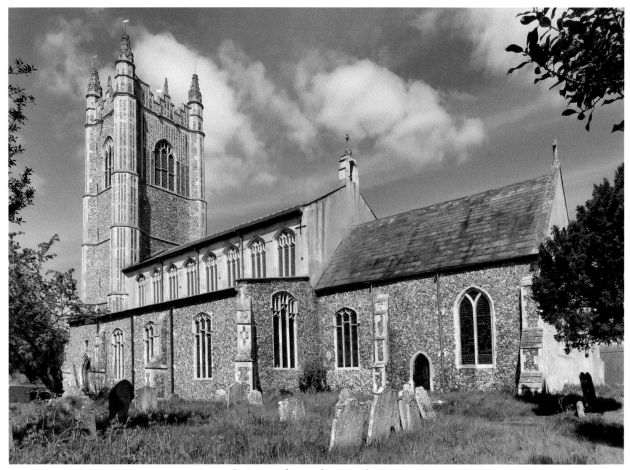

St Mary from the south east

St Mary dominates its surroundings from an elevated site, drawing eyes and admiration from all around. The C15th tower is one of the finest in East Anglia, a tour-de-force of assertive grandeur, with imposing octagonal buttresses, bold pinnacles, and double-step battlements. The stunning west face with its grand doorway is completely finished in flushwork, while the east and north face have it just on the belfry stages. The south face has flushwork only on the parapet. An earlier round tower was detected during excavations. Eight Perpendicular windows each side make up a lovely clerestory, while the north porch is no less ornate than the tower, with an upper room, flushwork, vaulted roof, niches and stoups by the entrance. Regrettably, a clear view of the church from most standpoints is impeded by unchecked trees and bushes. Inevitably, the interior falls short of the spectacular exterior, its medieval glories largely extinguished by a dull Victorian refurnishing scheme. Yet many items, not perhaps immediately noticed, are there to be found and admired. The inventory is surprisingly long. The font is a C19th version of a familiar C15th type, with angels and evangelist's symbols around the bowl and lions around the stem. While not universally liked, it is an admirable attempt to recreate an authentic medieval appearance. There is a good selection of wall tablets and other memorials, and many are grand affairs. Of particular note are the ones for members of the Kerrich family, but the most extravagant example is for Tobias Frere (d.1755) which stands near the monumental organ. A large but austere C16th tomb is mounted in the wall between the north (Gawdy) chapel and the C14th chancel. An old helmet is mounted above it in the chancel. The dado to the screen is C15th but a well-meaning attempt to repaint the panel figures was not successful. A great treasure and rarity is the double-headed eagle lectern of c.1500, burnished to a high polish and looking splendid. There is also a singular old wooden lectern. The Victorian glass is of mixed quality, none is of the highest rank. The Gawdy chapel has a window with heraldic glass and a pleasing reredos, both C18th. The royal arms is for Queen Anne. Two chests are of note, one is curious and crudely made, C15th, adorned with a motley set of paintings, including sailing ships, while the other is a fabulous C17th Flemish confection, with primitive-styled, exotic carvings.

The church from the east and south

North porch

Interior looking east and west

Chancel and sanctuary

Looking west from the sanctuary

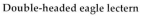

Double-headed eagle lectern

Simon Kerrich tablet (d.1748)

Gawdy tomb (C16th)

Flemish chest detail (C17th)

Roof boss

The font

South aisle window glass

Queen Anne royal arms

127

REEDHAM ST JOHN the BAPTIST

E3, TG 428 025

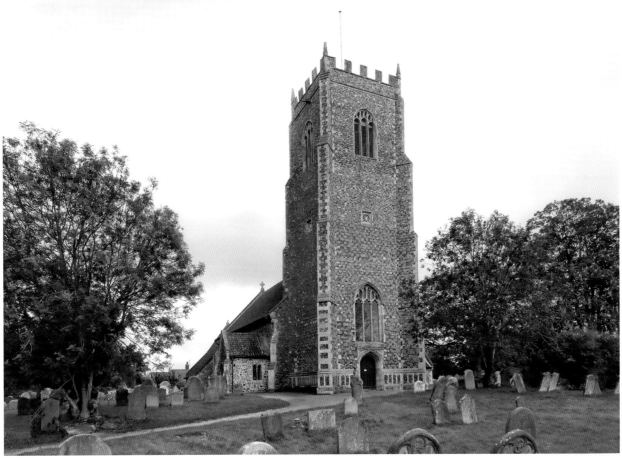

St John from the main approach from the north west

St John is a church with many tales to tell, and a very long, and recently disastrous, history. Despite the building being usually referred to the C14th and C15th, the amazing patchwork walls tell a more complex story. Particularly on the north side there are large areas of herringbone coursing typical of the years around the transition from Saxon to Norman architecture. What's more, the building material is Roman brick and tile, garnered from Roman buildings thought to have existed here. Random but abundant brick appears elsewhere in the walls. This suggests that some of the fabric at least dates back to 1100 or earlier, and its constituents very much further. The fabric also includes much medium-grained, grey stone in dressed blocks, and this appears to be Silver Carr, an uncommon type of Lower Cretaceous rock from west Norfolk, very rare in churches this far east. Yet there is lots of it here, this too was probably recycled from Roman buildings. The Romans of course built extensively and skilfully in stone and used Silver Carr in buildings nearer the outcrop. The C15th tower is finished in a subdued polytone chequerwork up to halfway, and once again Silver Carr is a major constituent. At the base is flushwork arcading. The west doorway has a square head and spandrel carving, and forms a feature with the west window. The east end is curious, there appears to be two chancels, under separate gables. The explanation is that there was once a south aisle, extended to create a chancel chapel. The aisle was later absorbed into the nave and its arcade removed, but the chapel remained. In the nave north wall is a blocked archway which may have led to a north chapel. A catastrophic fire in 1981 destroyed the roofs and interior, but a wonderful effort resulted in the church being refitted and open again within two years. Almost all the wooden fittings had to be replaced and the opportunity was taken to open up the interior to create a light, airy space. Of the old features, two splendid C16th tomb chests survived in the chapel, despite being baked. One is now unattributable, but the grander one of 1584 is for Henry Berney. A replacement medieval font was sourced from the redundant St Michael Coslany in Norwich. A nice Hanoverian royal arms is mounted above the south doorway. A beautifully aged silvered wood chest of 1720 stands at the west end. The modern glass in the two east windows is both accomplished and devotional.

128

Ancient walling

West doorway and window

Priest's doorway

Decorative beast

Looking east and west along the church

South chapel

The chancel

Ancient walling, interior

Doorway, chancel north

Old chest of 1720

Above the south door

Chapel east window

The font

Tomb chest c.1500

Henry Berney tomb, 1584

St Peter from the graveyard to the north

St Peter hides its attractions well and cannot be clearly seen from the road through the small village of Reymerston, it is necessary to walk along a pleasant, tree-lined ride to reach the entrance to the intimate and closely-set churchyard. Despite not being an especially large church, St Peter has a full plan of tower, nave, chancel and two aisles, with a modest clerestory, south porch and more recent vestry. The C13th tower is unadorned, with a plain top of 1714, and has Y-shaped belfry windows and a substantial stair turret to the north. Certain windows suggest that parts of the body of the church are also C13th, with some later Perpendicular work. The north doorway is Early English, with dogtooth. Inside, the C13th arcade piers have a range of capital designs, mostly stiff-leaf ornament, but all are tall and lend a stately air to the interior. The woodwork throughout the church is worthy of attention. The main nave roof is sturdy and unpretentious, and the aisles similarly have solid C15th timbers, though all the roofs have had subsequent restoration. The commanding pulpit is a focal point and is of 3-tier type, and has an associated family pew, also C17th. The panels are carved and the original impressive tester is still in place. Contemporary with the pulpit or perhaps a little later, are two rows of box pews in the aisles, and there is a typical small poor box, probably dating from the first half of the C17th. The exotic altar rails are of completely different origin and style, and characteristically flamboyant in the continental style of the C18th, they may be Flemish or French. The nave benches with their austere design and plain flat poppyheads have been attributed elsewhere to the C17th or even the medieval, but may be contemporary with the poor box, which is attached to the last bench of the north set. Equally, there is some debate as to the age of the distinctive nouveau-Gothic style choir stalls in the chancel, said to be either C18th or C19th. The east window has rather garish imported early C16th Flemish glass, showing large figures of St John the Evangelist, Christ and St Peter. The C15th font has assertively carved Evangelist's symbols and prophets with exaggerated wigs around the bowl, foliage beneath and fleurons on the stem. Of a small number of wall memorials, the biggest and best, of 1688 and in Latin, is for Robert Longe in the chancel. In the south aisle is the church's only brass, an inscription of 1509.

St Peter from the west and south   North doorway

Views around the interior

The font and nave   Pier capital   The pulpit   Box pews

Poor box   Longe memorial (1688)   Brimstone tablet (1796)   Tychepool brass of 1509

An elevated site adds to St Andrew's charms

To the west of Norfolk the churches thin out and like many others, Ringstead St Andrew has plenty of hinterland. But once the village could claim three churches. One of them, St Peter, was the original mother church, while another St Andrew was much smaller and lacked a tower. St Peter's round tower, though ruined, still stands in the garden of the old rectory; the shell of St Andrew stands in the outpost of Barret Ringstead. The two larger churches were consolidated in 1771, and St Peter allowed to ruin, some of its stone being used to repair St Andrew. Despite a rigorous Victorian makeover in 1865, St Andrew retains some older features. Externally, the thin tower was hit by lightning at some point and repaired on its south and west faces with brick, but the surviving Y-shaped belfry windows indicate a late C13th or early C14th origin. An old low-side window can be seen in the chancel south wall, probably C14th, as is most of the remaining original fabric. The very nouveau-Gothic and substantial north aisle was added in 1865, has its own gable and the east end is set aside for a vestry and organ chamber. The attractive porch with its statue of the Good Shepherd in a niche was renovated at the same time. This porch shelters an original C14th south doorway, with head stops. An almost entirely Victorian Gothic interior greets the visitor, and, as such, is worthy of study. The medieval is represented by a plain C15th font and an excellent angle piscina in the sanctuary, with plain drop-sill sedilia alongside. The piscina has beautifully moulded ogee arches, finials and heads. A simpler old piscina can be seen partly hidden by the pulpit, where there used to be a guild chapel. In the same area and associated with the chapel is an image niche, with ornate head. Preserved in the chancel floor is a tomb lid into which is set a fine figure brass. This is for Richard Kegill, a priest who ministered here and who died in 1482. Turning to the Victorian, the woodwork is of good quality and the low chancel screen is particularly attractive. At the rear of the nave benches is a charming poor box and nearby, a sturdy Victorian or somewhat earlier cupboard, presented in memory of a recent churchwarden. The decorative stone pulpit and ornate marble reredos are admirable pieces. The east window is by Frederick Preedy and shows the churches of St Andrew and St Peter held by their eponymous saints.

The church from the west and south

The porch

Interior looking west

Looking north east across the nave

The east end

North aisle, west end

A corner of the sanctuary

Angle piscina

Image niche

The font

Kegill brass (1482)

St Peter holds St Peter Ringstead

Victorian poor box

RUSHFORD ST JOHN the EVANGELIST

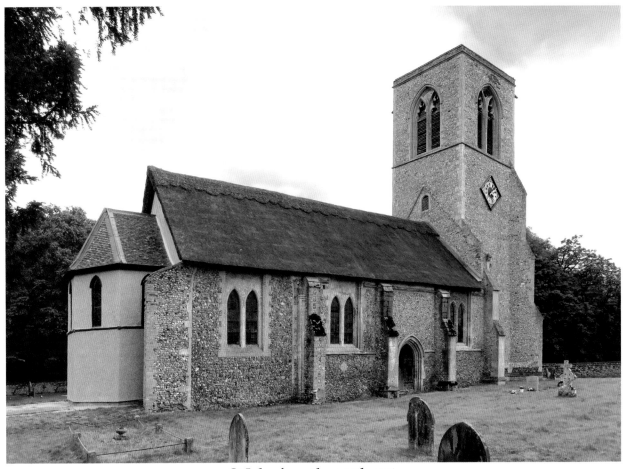

St John from the north east

The history and evolution of St John is full of interest, a fact not immediately apparent on first sight. It requires a careful examination of the outside to see that the fabric has much to tell. Most obvious is the curious toy apse at the east end, quite clearly not contemporary with the rest of the church. To either side of it are truncated walls and columns. Then it might be noted that on the north side there are quoins and columns in the wall of the nave at its east end. Over on the other side is a transept, but its fabric doesn't quite match the rest. And what is the meaning of the platform seen in the ground to the east of the apse? The line of an earlier and higher nave roof is marked out clearly on the east face of the tower, with a sanctus window beneath. Fortunately, St John's history is well-documented and these conundrums can be explained. In 1342 Edmund Gonville, the rector of St John, founded a college of priests very close to the church. His college building, in part, still exists today, a very rare and wonderful survival. Gonville's St John was cruciform in shape, with north and south transepts, also a large chancel. But hard times and the Reformation were ahead and in 1545 both transepts and the chancel were demolished (leaving the traces of their former existence described above), and other materials removed. The remaining shell was put to use as a barn, only to be restored as a church later in the C16th by the new owner Robert Buxton, who lowered the nave roof, inserted new brick windows and either built or remodelled the south porch. A vestry was built on the footprint of the south transept in 1889 and then in the early years of the C20th a sweeping reconfiguration transformed the church, initiated by the mother of the recently deceased John Henry Musker in his memory, which included the construction of the apse. Inside, a low flat ceiling was erected and the walls panelled, new dark furnishings were installed, possibly from nearby Brettenham, the walls were stencilled and a heavy devotional atmosphere was imposed on the interior. The lower sections of the medieval blank nave arcades and the arches and piers to the old transepts survive, also a ledger slab for a later Robert Buxton (d.1691), but no fittings of any age survive. The Caen stone font and pulpit, of similar style, are likeable, but the floor to ceiling screen is a little overbearing. The apse has been upgraded recently, and the hanging oil lamps are attractive.

St John the Evangelist from the north west, south east and east

Interior looking south east and north west   Screen and east end

The apse   Main organ & old transept arch   The pulpit   The font

Apse windows   Recent occupants of Rushford Hall   Hanging lamp   Pedal organ

The church from the north east

Following the pattern of a significant number of Norfolk, and indeed, East Anglian, churches, All Saints stands alone some way off to the north of its village, just off the B1140, and probably marks the site of the early medieval settlement. Since then, the village has migrated southwards and has developed into a fairly large community of some 1500 inhabitants, and has that rare thing, its own railway station. All Saints is mostly C14th, but much remodelling took place in the C19th. One of the first things to strike the visitor is the off-line, stumpy tower, which when built in the C15th was planned to be higher but work stopped when the money ran out. At the same time it was also projected to absorb the north aisle under an overall nave roof, which would have brought the tower into line with the nave, but that too was never done. Thus, a section of the tower arch, which was completed as part of the proposed work, is still exposed on the tower's east face. Nave and chancel are under one thatched roof, there is no chancel arch and the walls are low. The interior is very dark due to the lack of a clerestory and the small windows elsewhere, but flicking the light switches reveals an interesting layout and some intriguing features. The C13th arcade to the single north aisle has striking capitals, one with a series of mostly damaged heads and the others with a strong, fleshy leaf design. The screen and pulpit both retain some old sections, but the remaking of the screen in the C19th removed its character. However, it retains a very rare sanctus bell, mounted on top of the screen at the southern end. The cradle has been renewed, but the bell itself may be from the short reign of the Catholic Queen Mary, when for a brief period the Reformation was overturned. Mounted on the pulpit are a slightly less rare hourglass and holder, the glass itself is renewed. Easily missed in the chancel is an old misericord seat, with a bold face carved beneath. Locked away in the vestry is a C13th stone coffin lid. The C14th or C15th font came from Woodbastwick, and has a plain bowl which may once have been carved. There are several middling to good wall tablets, many for members of the Ward family, as are three funerary hatchments. A small palimsest brass is mounted on the nave south wall. The Victorian glass by Booker is excellent and there are two windows with melanges of medieval fragments. There are a few old bench ends with diverse poppyheads.

All Saints from the east, north west and west

Interior looking north east
Looking west from the sanctuary
Arcade capitals

The font
Some of the fine Victorian glass
And some medieval fragments
Late C18th Ward tablet

Mid-C19th Ward tablet/Palimsest brass
Old poppyheads
Ward funerary hatchment

All Saints is one of the smallest churches in East Anglia

Santon doesn't even qualify as a hamlet these days, yet the tiny church of All Saints is still in tidy and functional condition, having been looked after by its own preservation trust since the 1990's, when it was declared surplus to requirements by the Diocese of St Edmundsbury and Ipswich. It was the only church administered by that Diocese in Norfolk, but given that Santon lies just a stone's throw from the Suffolk border and is linked to nearby Santon Downham in Suffolk, that is hardly surprising. All Saints sits in the midst of the sombre Thetford Forest, in surroundings quite unlike those of any other Norfolk church. It lies at the end of a long, narrow lane, which only adds to the sense of detachment on arrival. All Saints is also in the running for the smallest church in East Anglia, and even the UK. Its survival into the C21st is due to the determination of successive incumbents and supporters, in the face of the ever shrinking village around the church. Once a possibly larger medieval chapel stood here, but by the early C17th it was largely derelict, at which point one of the few remaining parishioners (he may have been the only one), Thomas Bancroft, rebuilt the nave. And then in 1858 the incumbent, the Rev'd William Weller-Poley had a new chancel, porch and tower built, thereby creating the building seen today. He is buried in an ostentatious tomb chest immediately east of the chancel. Materials for Weller-Poley's building programme may have come from nearby West Tofts, when that church was being restored by the famous Augustus Pugin; there is some suggestion that Pugin himself may have contributed to the fitting out of the chancel. All Saints has no aisles, but to the south west is a vestry, and the miniature tower is built on top of this, creating an unusual configuration. The north porch is a cheerful and attractive feature, with pretty wooden weatherboarding and open sides. The churchyard is in keeping with the scale of the church, but seems to have lost many of its gravestones. A tour of the interior is quickly accomplished, but time should be taken to absorb the atmosphere and to study the best of the features. These include a small and neat C17th pulpit, probably the oldest item on view. The chancel is tiny, but everything is beautifully proportioned and sensitively ordered. The tiling behind the altar is striking and of high quality, and the roof is delightfully painted. Most of the glass is of early Victorian non-figurative type.

The porch

The church from the north

The diminutive tower

Interior views looking east and west

Tiny sanctuary

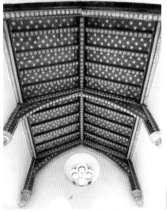

Chancel tiling

Chancel roof

Pulpit, commandment board

Victorian glass

East window

Chancel corbel

Vestry window

A beautiful sunny day shows St Mary to best advantage

St Mary is without doubt one of the finest churches in the area of Norfolk to the south of Norwich. Nearby are the ruins of another St Mary at Saxlingham Thorpe. The area all around is fine walking country, and several churches can be programmed into most enjoyable walks hereabouts. The church shows two very different faces to the world. The south frontage, the one most often seen, is beautifully balanced and looks its best in sunlight, but the northern aspect is cloaked in shadow and partly obscured by trees. A substantial north aisle of 1867 with gabled roof looms large, with unfortunate results for the aesthetics of the outline. The tower with its attractive chequerboard parapet is further distinguished by a superb large clock of 1794, which incorporates a sundial and is painted a fetching shade of blue. The west face features a stylish ensemble of large window with Perpendicular-style tracery, doorway and flushwork and at first may be taken to be old, but it is all very good Victorian work. The windows are mostly renewed, the nave and chancel are mostly C14th, but there may be older work. A low-side window forms the lower portion of a lancet in the south chancel wall. The south doorway is old and the door itself is clearly ancient, with two iron quatrefoils nailed onto it. To the right is a consecration cross and the remains of a holy water stoup. The glories for which St Mary is renowned are not immediately apparent inside, and the eye is first attracted by the fine C15th font, very boldly carved with lions and angels on the deep bowl and charming, smug lions around the stem. However, it is soon apparent that several windows contain exceptional and important collections of medieval and later glass. The sheer amount and diversity are astonishing, and despite the fragmentary nature of much of the material, there is a lot of figurative work. Four C13th roundels are the oldest figurative glass found in Norfolk and the rest ranges in age from C13th to C17th. Even the Victorian glass is notable. A visit to St Mary could be spent just studying this wonderful resource, but there are other delights to see. The panelling behind the altar is made from a C15th screen, presumably the original from the chancel. The C14th piscina nearby is mostly unrestored and is accompanied by drop-sill sedilia. Several good tablets adorn the walls, in particular an elaborate one of 1739 in the chancel. The royal arms is a very rare set for William III.

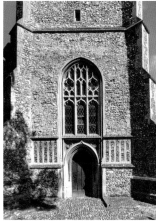
Tower west frontage

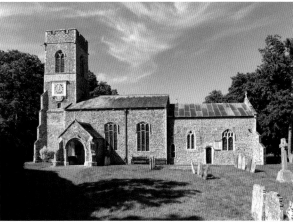
From the south

Porch and clock

Looking east and west along the church

The chancel and sanctuary

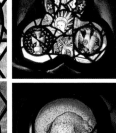

Examples of the rare and exceptional stained glass

The font

Two wall memorials (1739 and 1780)

William III royal arms

141

SCARNING ST PETER and ST PAUL

C2, TF 954 122

The church from the north east

Scarning is well placed for commuting to East Dereham and Norwich, and is very close to the main artery of the A47, thus it is no surprise that it has grown steadily from the days when the late C19th/early C20th incumbent Dr Jessop described the village as consisting of 'a few significant properties and 50 hovels'. These days around 2400 people make their homes here, and ensure that St Peter & St Paul is a well-cared for and supported church. The outline of west tower, nave, chancel and south porch is familiar, but as with all churches, there are a few notable features externally. The C15th tower has good flushwork on the base course, buttresses and parapets, the battlements are distinctively stepped and statues stand on the pinnacles. There are no aisles, but an unusually large late C16th transept springs off the chancel south wall, which once had an upper storey said to have been used as living quarters by members of the clergy. The noted architect Thomas Jeckyll did extensive work here between 1852 and 1859. He recorded that the commission was bedevilled by interference from the then rector, Rev'd Carson. The new work included reroofing, which involved lowering the walls; also new seating, pulpit and reading desk. Most windows were replaced, and there was some contention about Jeckyll's new east window, finished to an alien Decorated design. However, inside, Jeckyll retained the slim fluted jambs of the original. The excellent glass in the east window is by Wailes. The ambience of the interior is dictated by the cavernous nave, the dim chancel beyond the screen seeming tiny in comparison. Said screen is an excellent C15th example, restored and repainted, but retaining much of its medieval glory. Tucked away on the south east side, at the top, is an old sanctus bell with original handle but a later frame. The chancel contains most of the wall tablets of note, also a good piscina. An especially poignant tablet is for the unfortunate Edward Games, who died only 12 hours old in 1623. His tablet was made by the renowned Epiphanius Evesham. The lectern in the form of a pelican in her piety was copied from a medieval original in Norwich Cathedral. The royal arms of 1813 are for George III. The square font is a stunning late C12th or early C13th example with much archaic carving, and a handsome, painted Jacobean cover. The old rood stairs are concealed behind the organ.

The porch and tower

St Peter & St Paul from the north

The south doorway

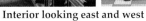

Interior looking east and west

Chancel and sanctuary

The C15th screen

….. and details

The font

The pelican lectern

George III royal arms

Edward Games memorial (1623)

Elizabeth Beevor tablet (1799)

St Andrew is a model of a well-loved church

Scole has long been a centre of population and an important crossroads, the Romans built a significant settlement here. The largely C14th St Andrew is neat and tidy, but not unduly exceptional, and the drama associated with it is unsuspected by the uninformed visitor. But on January 7th 1963 a local man took it upon himself to set fire to the church. Stalwart action by the fire brigade prevented complete destruction, but nearly everything wooden inside was lost, also the chancel arch and the roofs, including the C15th hammerbeam nave roof. In fact there wasn't a lot left that could be salvaged, and the collective hearts of the parish must have sunk. But not for long, rebuilding was rapidly put in hand and two years later the church was open again for business. New extensions built in the 1970's completed the renaissance, and today this is a church of which the people of Scole can be proud. Not perhaps for its external beauty, but the reconstructed interior has a welcoming ambience and is sensitively and comfortably fitted out, with kitchen, toilets and other amenities essential for a modern church. A few key features survived the fire, including some windows and the arcade with its low, early C14th piers, which are liberally adorned with graffiti. Among the latter are what appears to be a bishop (or soldier), and the inevitable initials. Above the arcade are the blocked windows of the clerestory. The fine C15th font also survived and is in splendid condition, maybe aided by some recutting. The bowl panels contain images of big-haired angels holding shields and banners. More angels are in flight beneath the bowl, and around the stem are cheery lions. A medieval angle piscina and its neighbouring sedilia are still in place in the aisle. An unexpected and welcome by-product of the fire was that restoration of the nave revealed a Norman window in the north wall, with traces of original painting. The nave seating largely survived the fire but was recently removed in favour of chairs. Traditional benches remain in the aisle and three of these have old bench ends with poppyheads. Apart from these remnants of the old church, the interior furnishings are all modern, and some are very good. In particular, the east window contains a striking and colourful abstract design by Patrick Reyntiens, who also designed glass for Coventry Cathedral. The aisle east window contains a more conventional 1920 design of the Resurrection by Edward Moore.

St Andrew from the west and north east   The porch

Looking east along the nave   The chancel   Interior looking west

Arcade and blocked clerestory   The Norman window   Piscina and sedilia in the aisle   The font

Reyntiens window (1965)   Moore window (1920)   Walker tablet, mid-C19th   Old bench end

All Saints fine lines are highlighted by winter sunshine

It is worth reiterating the merits, indeed the essential possession, of ordnance survey maps when visiting churches in Norfolk, and the rest of East Anglia for that matter. Here at Scottow, finding All Saints without one is a tortuous business, you may stumble upon it, but probably not. For a start, it lies quite some distance west of tiny Scottow village, buried in the huddle of buildings around Hall Farm, well off the nearest 'proper' road. On arrival there is the feeling of having trespassed onto a forbidden estate, but all is well, the largely C14th-C15th church is open to all. There is much to admire externally, a tall, slim tower and impressive porch with an upper storey and flushwork, both C15th. The porch has a vaulted roof with a splendid green man as a central boss, and there is a delightful priest's door to the chancel with ogee head and mutilated finial. There is no separate chancel, nave and chancel are under one roof, the distinction between them externally is marked by a prominent rood stair turret in the southern of the two aisles. The interior has many excellent fittings and features. There is no chancel arch but the division between nave and chancel is marked by the original rood beam. The font is a common Purbeck Marble type, but is a lot younger than it pertains to be. The C18th font cover is an extraordinary affair, with four green fish resembling sturgeons sporting happily. In the accustomed place on the arcade opposite the entrance is the bottom half of a medieval St Christopher painting. A later 'improving' black-letter text is painted on the arcade further east. A remarkable number of hatchments, most for the members of the Durrant family, adorn the walls. In the chancel is a C14th piscina with expressive, flowing tracery, now at ground level due to raising of the floor. Nearby is an early stone mensa conserved in a case. Also in the chancel is a small chalice brass of c.1520. As close as possible to the altar is the monolithic monument to Davy Durrant and wife, who died in 1759 and 1742, respectively. The box pews are late, installed as part of a Victorian restoration in 1858; the intricate, swivelling, two-sided lectern is C17th. The decidedly secular C17th wooden organ case is remarkable, carved with a bacchanalian extravaganza of figures, animals, foliage, cherubs and more. There are two royal arms, a huge (and rare) William III example and a handsome set for Elizabeth II, painted in C17th-C18th style.

Tower and porch

All Saints from the north west

Priest's door

Green man boss in the porch

The interior looking east and west

Mid-C18th Durrant memorial

Chancel piscina

Chalice brass, Nicholas Wethyrley 1520

Organ case detail

William III royal arms

St Christopher wall painting

Font and cover

Hatchments

All Saints from the south east

Unlike many Norfolk churches, the visitor will have no trouble in finding All Saints, which sits beside the main road through Shelfanger, the B1077. The pretty C14th tower, with flushwork parapet, red-tiled conical cap and sexfoiled 'sound-hole' is almost on the road and cannot be missed. Most of the church is C14th Decorated, with some later Perpendicular windows, but there is evidence of earlier foundation in the chancel, which will be discussed later. A highlight of the exterior is the outstanding north porch of around 1500, of a design rarely seen in Norfolk, consisting of a framework of wood infilled with split flints, raised on a flint wall base. It shelters a C14th doorway flanked by a time-worn holy water stoup that may pre-date it. An oddity is the position of the tower, which is set off to the north of the axis of the nave and chancel. The reason is not easily established, maybe the ground was unstable further south or perhaps the tower is on the footprint of an earlier tower of a church pre-dating the present one. The interior is smart and welcoming, but the Victorian makeover was perhaps a little too thorough, leaving few medieval items. However, there are some survivals of very special importance, a series of wall paintings on and adjacent to the chancel east wall. Their presence was unsuspected until 1965, when they were discovered in recesses behind a later wall. It was soon clear that they were of some significance, and they were restored to reveal, in particular, a beautifully executed nativity scene, dated as late C13th. That is on the south side, to the north the recess presents more mundane twining foliage, without figures (Tree of Life?). The font is a substantial C14th example, the bowl carved with tracery, the donor's coat of arms and initials (AB=Adam Bosville), which help date it accurately to the late C14th. Beneath the bowl are heads with portentous expressions. It seems that the east ends of both aisles were set aside as chapels, as both have drop-sill sedilia, and the southern one also has a nice piscina set into the window splay, with original credence shelf. In the same area is a contemporary image niche. The top section of the old Decorated rood screen with its varied tracery was recycled to form a frontage to the ringing gallery in the tower. Before leaving, see the sealed rood loft openings, old candle sconces on the walls, oil lamps, royal arms for Victoria and some decent Victorian glass by Clayton & Bell.

The church from the west and north west · The porch

Interior views to the east and west · The chancel · North east nave with sedilia

Tower arch screen detail · The font · South east nave piscina · Oil lamp

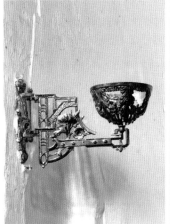   

Candle sconce · Nativity wall painting · Victoria royal arms · Glass by Clayton & Bell

SHOULDHAM THORPE ST MARY the VIRGIN B3, TF 661 080

St Mary's patchwork chancel is well seen in this view from the south east

St Mary is situated off a narrow lane in close-set countryside in mid-west Norfolk, but only a short distance away is one of the county's busiest roads, the A134. However, little of that is suspected as the visitor makes the pleasant approach along a sylvan path to this neat little church. It was rebuilt in 1858 by the prominent architect Anthony Salvin, who was faced with reconstituting a ruin. Much of the fabric consists of local carstone, but the lower part of the south east wall of the chancel contains courses of pale limestone, possibly recycled quoins from an earlier configuration. Some of this stone can be found in the chancel east wall too. Also in the chancel south wall is a rectangular area with an infilling which includes much ferrous conglomerate. Perhaps a chapel or vestry once stood here. The original building was probably Norman, with a tower, which fell around 1732 and also damaged the nave. The whole church later fell derelict, necessitating the mid-Victorian rebuilding. Some parts were recycled at that time, including the lovely Norman west doorway, which was originally the north doorway. Two C13th lancets in the chancel south wall were also retained from an early building. Both have rere-arches inside. A two-bell bellcote was erected on the west gable in 1858. A small lean-to vestry is located on the north side. The interior is quite plain with a simple and functional furnishing scheme, and at first glance there seems to be little of interest. However, a little investigating, as always, unearths some good things. On the chancel south wall is an old tablet that could very easily be overlooked, as it appears to have retained little detail. However, looking closely reveals three parts of what was presumably once a larger memorial, to Thomas Buttes, who died in 1600. Very indistinct now is a slab depicting the deceased praying at a prayer desk, in the Flemish fashion. The other significant wall memorial, which is in superb condition, is for three children of the Steuarde family, and dates from the very early C17th. The children are shown kneeling in a line beneath a strapwork head containing one big coat of arms and three smaller ones. The C14th octagonal font is a very presentable example with tracery patterns on the bowl. The openwork wrought iron candelabra hanging from the roof are attractive. There are a few minor features including a poor box and a nicely worked wooden collecting plate.

The bellcote

St Mary from the west

The Norman west doorway

Interior looking east

The chancel and sanctuary

Interior looking west

Poor box

Collecting plate

The font

West window glass

Steuarde memorial (early C17th)

Buttes tablet (1600)

Plaque for Jane Sophia (1898)

England's glory, St Mary at South Walsham

Church enthusiasts visiting the area north west of Acle tend to flock to the much-vaunted church of Ranworth St Helen, which indeed is worthy of the attention, but discerning visitors and those who shun the herd should consider turning their attention to South Walsham (and nearby Upton). Here they will find precious peace and wonderful churches to explore. There is special value at South Walsham, as there are two churches in the single churchyard. St Lawrence was almost destroyed by fire in 1827, but soon afterwards the chancel and a portion of the nave were restored for use. When the remains of the tower fell in 1970's, most assumed that was the end for St Lawrence, yet later in the 1990's it was brought back from ruination and rebuilt as a centre for training and the arts. Thus, St Mary has for some time been the only 'working' church in South Walsham, and an excellent one it is, mostly C14th-C15th. The impressive exterior of the church is distinguished by an imposing C15th tower, two aisles and a splendid south porch, with parvise. Its south face is beautified by a handsome doorway with spandrel carvings of the Annunciation, and, above, a niche containing a carving of the Coronation of the Virgin, flanked by two windows which were probably themselves once niches. In the south west corner of the chancel is a low-side window. There is lots to see inside. The C14th font with medieval tiles around its stem has pretty tracery in its bowl panels, and behind it under the tower arch is a mighty late C18th organ. Both rood loft openings are still in place, complete with stairs, and to the north of them is a mostly original C15th screen, its panels painted with floral motifs and a dedication to the donor, John Galt. Some nave benches contain C15th or C16th elements, particularly ends with arm rest carvings and poppyheads, some bearing shields. At least five inscription brasses survive, the only one in English dating from 1638. There are two good wall tablets, one records a benefaction by Christopher Harrold (1766) and the other is for members of the Jary family (early C19th). The sanctuary contains part of a large C15th grave covering, an incised coffin lid, banner stave niche and two (or three) aumbries, and the customary piscina and sedilia, all medieval. Also an old chest. A rare double aumbry can be seen beside the north aisle altar. The C19th and C20th glass by the William Morris workshop and R. O. Pearson is excellent.

St Mary from St Lawrence   St Mary from the north west   The porch

Interior looking east   Font and organ   Chancel east end   Rood loft doorways

Lower rood loft doorway   The screen   Screen detail   The sower

Brasses   Poppyhead and bench end   Jary tablet

153

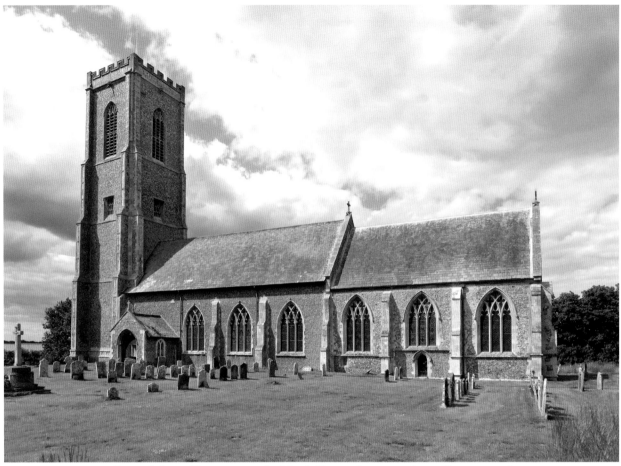

One of the tallest towers in Norfolk can be seen for miles around

Here is a wonderful, big church whose C15th tower dominates the surrounding area. The rest of the largely C14th church is appropriately in scale and the whole building must have awed the people of Norfolk when the two aisles demolished in 1791 were still in place. Even without them, this remains a most impressive building, which replaced an original Norman church, probably in the C14th. No expense was spared on the tower, which is embellished, particularly on the west face, with flushwork, niches, ornate friezes featuring the scallop shell emblem of St James the Greater, and a powerful west window. The doorway below the latter is a tour-de-force and beautifully realised. There is a south porch, vestry and modern northern extension, built in 1995. The interior is a vast, booming space, and even with a generous range of furnishings, looks rather sparsely filled. However, the building is beautifully maintained, well loved and supported. The area beneath the tower was recently converted into a comfortable social space. Sadly, the interior was expunged of most of its medieval fittings during restorations in 1875 and 1908. The medieval origins of the church are best seen in the chancel. Here there is a super priest's doorway in the south wall adorned with fine heads set on either end of the hoodmould and on the string course to either side. The doorway is dated around 1320. That is also the date suggested for the butchered piscina and sedilia further east, the latter reduced to one and a half arches. Despite the truncation the arches are still impressive, with intricate ornamentation. Other C14th details include slim pillars with foliated capitals to the rere-arches of the windows, and headstops. There is a low-side window containing medieval glass depicting a seraph. The Victorian glass is good. In the nave both arcades to the vanished aisles remain and confirm a C14th age. The font is an unexceptional C14th or C15th item, with quatrefoils on the bowl. The screen retains much C15th detail, especially the panels, painted green and red with little flowers and Marian monograms. Wall tablets include a slightly macabre early C18th memorial to Barton husband and wife, and two early C19th tablets, an oval one for the Bond family and a large tablet for the Rev'd Charles Smith. The royal arms is for George III and an old parish chest stands near the font. There are two old inscription brasses and another from 1862 should be seen.

St James from the east and north east　　　　　Tower west doorway

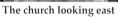

The church looking east　　　The chancel　　　The nave looking west　　　Priest's doorway

Sedilia　　　　　The font　　　　Screen, north side　　　Brasses (1598, 1608, 1862)

Barton tablet　　Smith, Bond tablets: Royal arms　　Medieval glass and C19th glass by Mayer & Co, Munich

155

SPARHAM ST MARY the VIRGIN

St Mary from the south west

St Mary is a lovely church, packed with interest. It is a mixture of C14th and C15th elements, but the low, narrow chancel may be earlier. There was a major reconfiguration and enlargement of the church in the C15th, and for the buildings historian, that left much to conjure with. At that time the nave was heightened to accommodate a clerestory, and two smaller blocked windows at the east end of the arcades are thought to be the vestiges of an earlier and lower clerestory. However, there are no traces of other windows running west from them, so they may have been left to light the rood, which was also the function of the exceptionally large gable window. At the west end two tower buttresses impinge into the aisles, leading to the suggestion that the then new tower was free-standing for a while until the building was extended westwards to meet it. It seems the builder's mathematics were awry, because the arcades then had to be configured with two wide bays to bridge the gap, which did not match the others. The real story may never be known. The interest doesn't end with the evolution of the building, the interior is filled with intriguing items. The C15th screen was long ago dismantled but four panels remain, now housed in the north aisle, and two of them depict exceptionally rare and vividly morbid *momento mori*. St Thomas of Canterbury and St Walstan appear on the other two. Another rarity, a brass of c.1493, shows William Mustarder in full priestly vestments; other inscription brasses are nearby. The C15th nave roof has angels at the intersection of the principals and corbels with angels holding shields. There is much old woodwork in the form of bench ends with poppyheads, and one bench end carving, of a dog. The altar rails are pre-C19th, and the pulpit retains some medieval elements. The western arch of the chancel angle piscina is broken and the aperture sealed; further west are unusual arched recesses with stone seats, perhaps originally for priests. The south aisle also has a piscina. Both rood loft openings survive. The royal arms is for George I. A nice chair of 1871 in C17th style and a pretty ?C18th sideboard with geometrical carving are worth seeking out, but not the dull C19th font. A much-abused ancient holy water stoup is situated by the south doorway. In 2008 beautifully designed stained glass by Emma Blount in the shape of a Tree of Life was set in the north aisle east window.

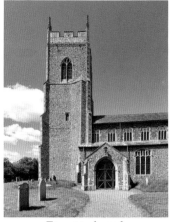
Tower and porch

The church from the north east

Nave gable window and chancel

Interior looking east and west

The chancel

Rood loft openings

Chancel piscina and sedilia

Rare and fabulous medieval screen panels

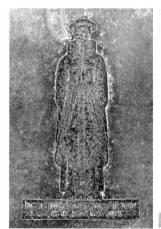
Mustarder brass, late C15th

George I royal arms

Bench end dog

The font

St Mary from the north

Stalham is a large, busy and popular village in the northern Norfolk Broads tourist area, and, as such, is often thronged with traffic. That imparts an urban feel, and that impression is carried over into St Mary. Stalham being a prosperous place, at least since the C19th, the availability of local money has meant that the church, and particularly its interior, was frequently revamped, and, because of that, perhaps a certain lack of harmony is apparent inside. However, that impression is largely offset by the excellent medieval features and fittings that were retained. The church probably began life in the C13th, but, as in so many cases, C14th and C15th building campaigns overprinted the earlier work and what we see today is largely a building created in those centuries. The C15th tower was never completed and remains low and squat. The tiny quatrefoil clerestory windows to the south replaced earlier two-light ones which were partly obscured when the south aisle was built; the two-light windows were then blocked. The aisles are typical C14th work with a low profile and lean-to roofs. The east windows of both have attractive flowing tracery. The south porch is C15th and was restored in the C19th. One of the highlights of the interior is immediately apparent to visitors, and that is the very fine C15th font. It is beautifully preserved, and the figures on the bowl panels escaped attack by iconoclasts because the contemporary church authorities wisely plastered over them. In the C19th the exquisite carvings, comprising six pairs of Apostles, Christ's baptism and the Holy Trinity, were re-exposed. Around the stem are prophets and saints, and the whole is raised on three steps, the top two elegantly ornamented. The medieval screen was removed long ago, but five panels depicting saints were kept, restored and are now mounted on the south chancel wall. In front of the altar are two small, C15th brass figures, a man and his wife. Nearby is an extravagant chest tomb for Katherine Smyth (1718); part of the chest on the left hand side is missing, but the top half is complete. Around the junction of the north aisle and chancel arch is an excellent rood stair, leading to the open upper opening. Mounted at the base of the chancel arch north pier is a grave marker and crest from 1661. In the south chapel is a nice ensemble of angle piscina and drop-sill sedilia. Near the south door is an elaborate holy water stoup, with pillar drain and ornate square head.

158

St Mary viewed from the north east, south and south east

Interior looking east   Looking north west across the nave   The south chapel

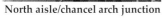

North aisle/chancel arch junction   Chancel arch pier memorial   Rood loft stairs   Smyth chest tomb (1718)

The font   Angle piscina in the south chapel   Man and wife brass   Rood screen panels

STRUMPSHAW ST PETER

D3, TG 349 077

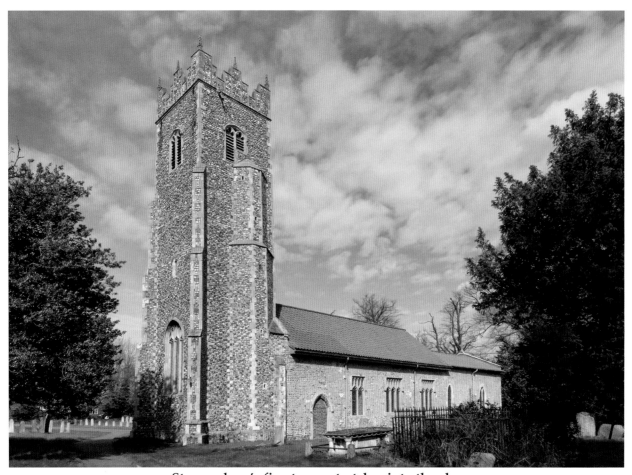

Strumpshaw's fine tower stretches into the sky

Strumpshaw is best known for its bird reserve, which has vistas of sweeping, atmospheric marshland inhabited by many fascinating wild creatures, but the church of St Peter is also worth a visit. Before inspecting the fine interior, there are some interesting things to see externally. Firstly the grand tower for which bequests were left in 1485–1487, it has an excellent flushwork panelled parapet and stepped battlements, prominent south exterior stair turret and buttresses as far as the last stage. The Early English chancel is probably the oldest part of the church and has lancet windows both sides and a priest's doorway. The north porch was heavily restored in the C19th. There are no aisles. The nave has a set of handsome Perpendicular windows. The churchyard is extensive. Entry is via the north door, the southern doorway is sealed with brick. The font, with shields and tudor roses on the bowl, is C15th; there are angels with mutilated faces beneath the bowl and lions around the stem. Flanking the font, set in the floor, are two smart ledger slabs, and several others can be seen elsewhere in the nave. On walls nearby are a George III royal arms and a wooden benefaction board dated 1755. On the south wall opposite the north door is one of several striking wall tablets in St Peter, this one for Edward Smith who died in 1812. Elsewhere are even better tablets for William Springall (1757), members of the Barnes family (late C18th), Catharina Nelson (1789), Mary Redhead (1811) and Edmund Whitbread (1868), plus a few minor memorials. Near the screen are three inscription brasses, with clear but almost unreadable gothic script, probably C15th or early C16th. All begin with 'Pray for the soul of ….'. A fine C15th chancel screen survives, with undecorated rectangular areas on the nave side with stanchions, indicating the previous presence of altars for chapels north and south. The painting where present is of stencilled flowers and monograms on red and green backgrounds. The chancel possesses a superb Early English piscina and sedilia set. The double piscina has beautifully moulded trefoil arches, typically slim piers, and head stops, one a lizard amongst foliage. The sedilia are stepped. Both rood loft openings are extant, the upper blocked, but the lower retains its stairs. The nave south wall has an empty tomb niche, and a tall banner stave locker is located near the north door.

160

From the south east   St Peter from the north   On the tower roof

Interior looking east   The chancel   Interior looking west   Rood loft openings

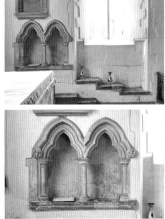

The rood screen   The font   Piscina and sedilia   Springall tablet (1757)

Redhead tablet (1811)   Three inscription brasses   George III arms. Benefaction board   Stained glass

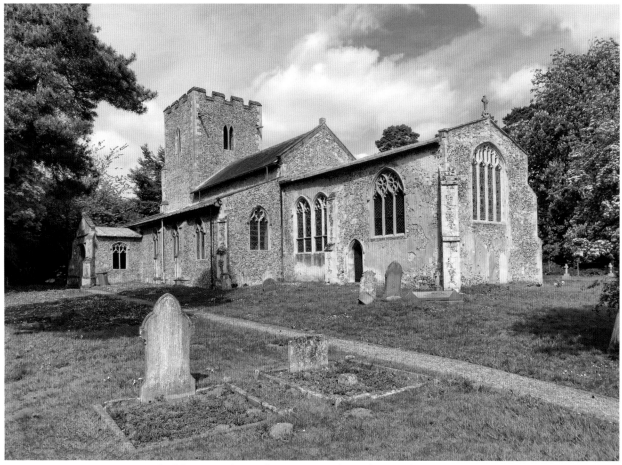

St Margaret is set in an attractive elevated position

St Margaret is an open, welcoming church with an array of excellent features both inside and out, pleasantly set above the scattered village of Swannington. The church has C13th features like the north and south doorways, the north aisle was built around 1300, and the chancel somewhat earlier. The south aisle may be mid-C14th. The stout C14th or C15th tower was constructed inside the pre-existing nave and is open internally, with arches to the nave and enclosing aisles, which gives an airy and spacious feel to the west of the church. The south porch is Perpendicular and has a notable south façade, with flushwork crowned lettering at the base and the legend *ihs nazarenus* above the arch. In the spandrels are lively scenes showing St Margaret's encounter with a dragon. By the south door is a battered holy water stoup. Off the nave north west wall and accessed through the north door is an early 1980's extension, housing modern facilities. Further improvements inside were made in 2009. The south door leads into the large space beneath the tower, and to the east of the aisle arch is a large mural of St Christopher. Nearby in the south aisle is a time-worn C13th font, of familiar Purbeck Marble type, the bowl shallow and carved with paired arches. The west window of the south aisle has old glass in its tracery, including a rather eroded Norwich School angel as a centrepiece. The eye-catching glass in the chancel east window is unusual, most of it of foreign origin. Much of it consists of floral and foliage patterns, but there are two very striking portraits of Jesus and John the Baptist. The style suggests a late C18th or early C19th age. The triple sedilia and piscina nearby are admirable, the former has carvings of a variety of leaves at the head of the arches, and the latter incorporates a pillar piscina, with a Norman capital as a bowl. This is carved with vivacious scenes of St George and the Dragon and a battle depicting a textbook Norman shield and equipment. The beautifully carved communion table is dated 1635 but the handsome altar rails, though traditionally styled, are probably Victorian. The arcade piers are heavily inscribed with ancient grafitti but angled light is necessary to see it well. In brief, see also the chancel and north aisle medieval roofs, recessed and arcaded sedilia in the chancel north wall, a George III royal arms and hatchments in the north aisle, and piscinas in both aisles signifying the former presence of chapels.

St Margaret pictured from the east and north east

The south porch

Interior looking east

The chancel

Interior looking west

North aisle roof

Rood loft openings

Chancel piscina and sedilia

The piscina and its bowl

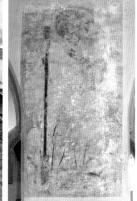

The font

St Christopher painting

Early C19th? and medieval glass

Communion table/George III arms

The felling of a big tree recently unveiled this view of St Edmund from the north east

Norfolk has many isolated, atmospheric churches, but for distinctive 'feel' Swanton Novers St Edmund takes some beating. It possesses a singular, mysterious aura which emanates from its setting at the end of a long narrow lane in close, timeless countryside. The building itself plays its part because of the unmistakeable signs of great age in its fabric. It is rare to see obvious signs and dimensions of an original C11th church, but there are three sets of quoins, two at the western end of the nave and one at its eastern limit in the southern wall, which delineate the extent of the nave of the first stone church on this site. Remarkably, the nave was never extended and is still marked off by the same quoins today. The 'missing' set from the east end of the north wall is probably concealed by the C19th north aisle. These quoins are made with large, irregular chunks of ferrous conglomerate, which is usually taken to indicate Saxon or perhaps early Saxo-Norman work. Evidence of a semi-circular headed doorway in the nave south wall also supports an early origin for St Edmund, but too little original fabric remains to allow more constrained attribution. The building was revamped at various times over ensuing centuries, but the most significant changes came in the C19th, when the chancel was rebuilt, the north aisle added and the interior reconfigured. The chancel walls externally are remarkable, being a melange of different stones recycled from previous chancels (including dressed stone from the framework of windows), together with more familiar flint and much 'found' material. The addition of polychrome heads to the windows add a further unexpected touch. Inside, almost all is Victorian. The C15th font was kept, with its shields, Evangelist symbols and angels beneath the bowl. It is also engraved with a curious 'W' or double 'V' monogram, which is also carved twice on the ornate C15th piscina in the chancel. It most likely refers to important donors, who probably provided many other items in the church, now long gone. Although difficult to justify, on the website of the benefice of which Swanton Novers is a part, it is said that the letter is an 'N' and that it refers to the De Noers family, who gave their name to the village. There are a few wall tablets and the Perpendicular-styled arcade is elegant, but the best of the later features is the fine stained glass of 1888 in the nave south wall window, commemorating Margaret Chambers.

St Edmund from the south
The patchwork chancel
South west quoin

The interior looking east
The chancel
Chancel south east

The interior looking west
The font
Chancel piscina
Close-up of the lettering

Wall tablets
War memorial
Brass memorial
Stained glass window in the nave

St Mary from the south east

Swardeston and its church are irrevocably associated with the 1st World War hero, nurse Edith Cavell, shot by the Germans in 1915 for treason. She was born here, her father was vicar and she worshipped in St Mary, and ever since her death, the village and 'her' church have been places of pilgrimage for thousands of people. St Mary merits the attention, for it is an ancient, dignified place. There are no great treasures, but all is calm and peaceful. The origin of the building goes back to the time around the Conquest, when the double-splayed, round-headed windows in the nave north and south walls were emplaced. The bricks in their heads may be Roman. Nave and chancel are contained under one roof and there are no aisles. The tower, embellished with flushwork parapet and battlements, and long external stair turret, is C15th. The agreeable south porch has inner and outer doorways made of Tudor brick, and has a tablet set into a niche above the outer doorway. The interior is light, neat and well cared-for. At a time when many churches were disposing of Victorian pews in favour of more comfortable chairs, St Mary went the other way in 1977 and removed chairs in favour of pews obtained from St Margaret at Westwick in Norwich. The wood for the screen dado came from the same source. The rest of the smart screen is original C15th work; its paintwork was renewed in the 1990's and the hybrid screen makes a fine feature. The hoary font, starkly plain, is said to be C14th, but is completely eclipsed by its C17th wooden cover, an excellent example of sturdy, rustic carving. It is thought that the equally solidly built altar rails are the work of the same craftsman. The nave roof, of king-post and tie-beam construction, though restored, is old and attractive. At the base of the nave walls are rows of arched recesses, now empty, but which probably once housed tombs or burials. The nave walls have other curious features, seemingly the vestiges of door and window openings. The chancel boasts a fine ensemble of features in its south east wall, consisting of aumbry, angle piscina, sedilia and a niche housing the remains of a pillar piscina. There are some fragments of medieval glass, also a few C17th Flemish roundels. The east window glass commemorates Edith Cavell. The chancel contains a suite of benches with old ends, exuberant poppyheads and bevels decorated with fleurons. The royal arms are for George II.

The south porch

The church from the south west

Saxo-Norman window

Interior looking east

The rood screen

The chancel

Looking west from the sanctuary

Lots of interest in the chancel

Vestiges of the rood loft

Font and cover

Chancel furniture

Nave roof

Glass of various ages

George II royal arms

Moxon tablet, late C18th

St Mary with the Harvey mausoleum to the left

Despite the presence nearby of busy Long Stratton and the incessant traffic of the A140, around Tharston all is peace and rural calm. St Mary may once have stood at the centre of a more populous village, but these days it enjoys a tranquil existence with only a farm or two for company. A church here is mentioned in the Domesday Book and it is possible that some of the dressed limestone blocks in the fabric of both chancel and nave, both rectangular and cylindrical, were recycled from that early building. The chancel dates from around 1300 and was rebuilt by Ewan Christian in 1864, the nave was rebuilt in the mid-C15th and again in the late C19th by Richard Phipson, whilst the tower and porch are both late C15th or early C16th and were restored by E.P. Willins in 1886. There are no aisles. The tower buttresses, parapet and base course, and the porch, all exhibit nice flushwork; the porch's patterning, dominated by verticals, is especially attractive. The tower west doorway has a square head with Tudor roses in the spandrels, a theme echoed on the font inside. The graveyard contains the mausoleum of the Harvey family of 1855. The C15th font greets visitors as they enter, it has bold carving of lions and Tudor roses on the bowl, also angels bearing shields, but the benign lions around the stem steal the show, they are full of character. The angels with intertwined wings beneath the bowl were singled out for particularly harsh treatment by iconoclasts. On the walls are several notable memorial tablets, some of which are for members of the Harvey family, the same that built the mausoleum outside. See especially the one for Sir Robert Harvey of 1860, with two prominent Peninsula War soldiers. His wife also has a rather grand marble tablet (1869). Also of interest is an impressive tablet for Robert Woode and wife of the 1640's which depicts Robert as a gruesome skeleton on his death bed. Another large tablet for members of the Woode family dates from the 1760's. See also the tablet for John and Alice Woolmer (early 1600's) and the excellent C20th war memorial. The belfry rail is part of a set of early C18th altar rails originating from St Margaret of Westwick (Norwich). Three old bench ends (restored 1928) have superb carvings, including St Michael weighing souls and the Assumption of the Virgin Mary; excellent poppyheads too. The chancel has a good piscina, but no sedilia. The reading desk is made from recycled Jacobean panels.

St Mary from the south west and north west

The tower from the south east

Interior looking east

Interior from the chancel

The sanctuary

The font and detail with cheery lions

Chancel piscina

Bench ends and poppyhead

Reading desk

Woode tablet (1640's)

Memorials of Sir Robert and Lady Charlotte Harvey (1860, 1869)

169

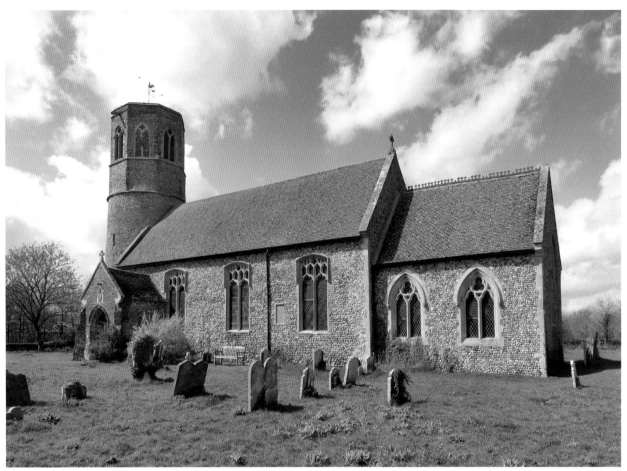

A sparkling May day at Thorpe Abbotts

Thorpe Abbotts All Saints is a church for the buildings detective, as the fabric is full of riddles and clues to the evolution of this ancient church. Many are very subtle, and are easily missed, but vital to the story. It is likely that some of the clues take the story back into Saxon times, for instance in both nave walls beneath the westernmost windows are two indistinct lines of crude flint quoins. These quoins define the western end of an original nave. At the other end of the nave on the north side is a much better defined set of the same type demarking the eastern end of this nave. In between the two north nave windows is a blocked, round-headed doorway, with a head constructed of the same crude flints as the quoins. All of these features could be Saxon work, using the materials at hand, in this case flint. Later builders most often used imported, dressed stone for their quoins. The chancel has seen several reconfigurations, but it is likely that it occupies part of the same footprint as an original Saxon chancel and may retain some contemporary fabric. There is faint evidence of a break in fabric style about two thirds up the nave, and possibly chancel, walls and this may represent the heightening of a Saxon building. Most round towers are generally, but not universally, accepted to be of Saxon or Norman origin, but here that seems unlikely, because if the tower was contemporary with the nave, it would have stood some way away from it. It may be that the nave was extended west, perhaps in the C13th or C14th, and a tower built at the same time. The presence of bricks in the tower fabric, unless they are recycled Roman bricks, would seem to confirm a C13th or later age, because bricks were not 're-invented' in England until that time. The exterior is fascinating, but there is more of interest inside. The C15th font is in amazing condition, due to being plastered over in the C16th or C17th, and not revealed again until the C19th. It shows Evangelist's symbols, fine angels and other devices. The screen is also C15th, has excellent Perpendicular tracery and incorporates the old rood beam. The super east window glass of 1868 is by Ward & Hughes, nearby are the arms of Bury Abbey in much older glass. The chancel roof is mostly medieval, and was beautified further by the addition of beatific wooden angels in the C19th. The royal arms are those of George III. The set of oval wall tablets for members of the Kay family is attractive.

  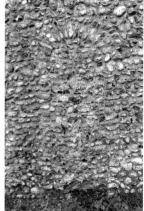

All Saints from the north and south west   Blocked ?Saxon doorway

Interior looking east   The rood screen   The east end   Interior looking west

Chancel roof   ….. and angel   George III royal arms   Kay family tablets

Lest we forget ….   East window detail   Arms of Bury Abbey   The font

All Saints from the north west

All Saints is a likeable little church with lots of excellent features, inside and out. Like all churches it has seen its share of reconfigurations and changes, but the south doorway leaves no doubt as to its origins. This is a fine example of Romanesque artistry, with characteristic semi-circular head with four orders of mouldings, all different, and two shafts each side with cushion capitals. The north doorway, protected by a most agreeable porch enriched with brick inlays, flushwork and a niche in the gable, and square headed entrance arch with shields in the spandrels, also demands attention. It is very ornate with an inner moulding enhanced with crowns (most sadly mutilated), whilst the hoodmould has little fleurons and big angel stops, with a carving of the Trinity at the apex. Censing angels occupy the spandrels. The door itself, with its Perpendicular tracery, is contemporary with the doorway. The C15th tower has a handsome west face with a chequer pattern at the base and a panelled flushwork frieze above; a similar design adorns the parapet. The chancel is C13th on the evidence of some primitive coursing and a lancet window to the north. Most other windows are Perpendicular. Inside, both tower and chancel arches are exceptionally tall, with thin, spindly mouldings. The C15th font has Tudor roses and shields on the bowl, with a flight of angels beneath. None of that ornament is particularly mutilated, and strangely it was the innocuous lions around the stem that came in for most abuse from the fundamentalists. The C15th screen is the high point of the interior, despite losing much of its dado panelling. The tracery above is finely wrought and is painted red, green, black and gold, with lovely little flowers twining up the two centre posts. The chancel is simply laid out, with little in the way of extravagance. There is no piscina or sedilia, and the altar is a plain old table, but the brick floor, which also extends to the sanctuary, adds character and there are some substantial ledger slabs. The organ is an individual piece, but the best items in the chancel are the wall memorials, particularly two for members of the Denny family. One is a striking cartouche of 1717 and the other of 1665 is a bold and elegant tablet, with a broken pediment framing an impressive shield. On the north nave wall is a very large St Christopher painting, and lower down what may be a piscina. In front of the screen is a naïve brass inscription of 1646.

All Saints from the south west

North porch

South doorway

North doorway

Interior looking east

Screen and chancel

Looking west from the chancel

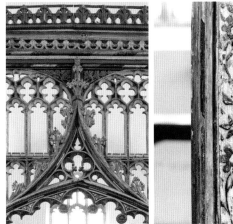
Screen details

Brasses 1646 and 1902

The font

Ann and Margaret Denny memorials, 1665 and 1717

St Christopher wall painting

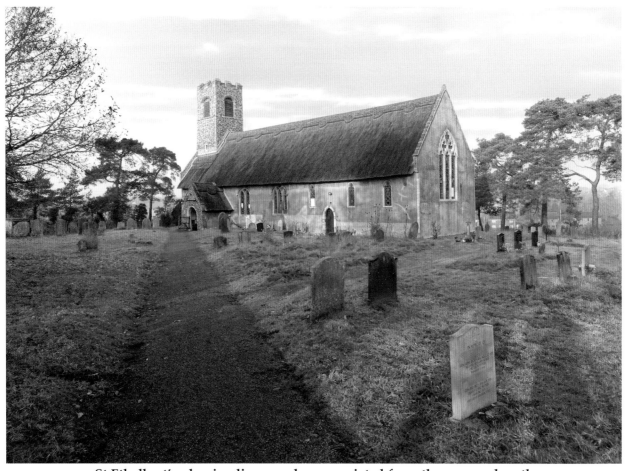

St Ethelbert's pleasing lines can be appreciated from the approach path

St Ethelbert is a familiar sight to motorists driving south on the busy A146, sitting prettily on its hill overlooking Thurton. Close up, it is just as pretty and its classic one-cell C12th Norman outline is immediately apparent, suitably enhanced by the fine thatched roof. The building has been modified over the years with later windows, but the antiquity of the structure is amply demonstrated by the markedly leaning north wall and the deep internal splays on several windows. If there was any doubt as to the origins, it is dispelled by the two main doorways. The southern one is the best and most ornate, and indeed is one of the best Norman examples in Norfolk, with four orders of mouldings in the arch and three slim piers to the sides, with scalloped capitals. It is probably no coincidence that the classic Romanesque doorways of Hales and Heckington are not far away. The north doorway, as is usual, is simpler, with only one order of billet moulding in the hoodmould. The configuration of the tower is unusual, it was partly enclosed by the nave at some stage, creating two narrow rooms north and south of the tower, accessed via low doorways in the nave. The result of that modification is that the section of the tower above the nave resembles an extended bellcote, but that is an illusion, the tower remains entire to ground level. Unsurprisingly, the interior has the feel of a barn, but a very intriguing one. However, the small, plain, octagonal font is unexceptional, and apart from being post-medieval, is hard to date. It may be contemporary with the neat C17th altar rails, with their balusters and square newels. A large ?C15th wall painting of St Christopher on the north nave wall is very obscure in its upper parts, but clearly seen in the water at the Saint's feet a variety of crustaceans are sporting. Other wall paintings can be seen on the nave walls, all are in poor condition and difficult to decipher, but intriguing faces peer out here and there. Mounted over part of one of them is an inscription brass of 1631. Two wall tablets in the chancel to members of the Margerum family are the only significant memorials. There is much excellent and rare stained glass, most installed by S. C. Yarrington in 1826. A very fine Trinity is the only medieval image, but the C16th – C18th foreign pieces are exceptional, as are depictions of saints and other subjects by Robert Allen, better known as a ceramic painter at the Lowestoft factory.

St Ethelbert from the north west   The south doorway   The north doorway

Looking east   The chancel at Christmas   Interior looking west

Gouldworth brass (1631)   Margerum tablet (early C19th)   The font   St Christopher and another painting

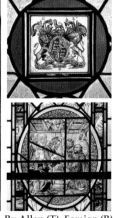

By Robert Allen (late C18th)   By Allen (T), Foreign (B)   Foreign (from Rouen Cathedral?)   Medieval Trinity

St Mary from the south west

Thwaite St Mary stands some distance from settlements of similar size, and there are no other churches close by. That isolation has generated an independent and self-sufficient air to the village. Its church of St Mary has a number of things in common with the preceding church, Thurton St Ethelbert, particularly similarities between the naves. Both are Norman, aisleless, long and low, with thatched roofs, and both can boast an exceptionally good Romanesque south doorway. Thwaite's is the showier of the two and has more lavish ornamentation, there is expressive and varied carving on almost all the surfaces. The arch, with seven orders of mouldings, is especially fine. A much-worn but characteristic beakhead is mounted above the apex, and hints that there may once have been corbel tables below the nave roof, similarly adorned. The tower, which may have replaced a round one, is C14th and has an unusual ornament of three blank shields in a frame, above a small brick-lined niche on the west face. The chancel dates from 1737 and is also in brick and, like the nave, has no windows on the north side. The nave once had at least one of lancet type, confirmed by a splayed opening inside, and there were possibly more. The west window on the south side is flanked by two memorial tablets. Inside, all is neat and ordered, but little survives of great age. Interestingly, some of the chancel furnishings from the 1737 rebuilding are still in place, notably the rather stark Georgian screen, with its trefoil heads, which seems to incorporate parts of an older frame. The chancel has no sedilia or piscina in the traditional sense, but an old bowl, perhaps from an earlier piscina, is set in the usual position, but is possibly just for show. The chancel roof is painted blue and is distinguished by crossing timbers. Several metal and stone memorial plaques and tablets are dotted around, but, again, none are very old. The plaque of 1848 for two sisters, set in the frame of the east window, makes interesting reading. The plain font bowl has a post-medieval look, but is mounted on an older stem. The only stained glass is in the east window, and is undistinguished. Four roundels salvaged from a bomb-blasted earlier window are reset here. A lovely old chair stands near the pulpit, and is possibly C18th. In the splay of the blocked north nave window is an old painting of Mary and the Christ-child, but attribution and origin are unknown.

St Mary from the west and north east

The south doorway

The interior looking east and west

The west end

The sanctuary

Old woodwork in the screen

Old chair

The font

Piscina bowl

Plaques

Reeve tablet (1832)

Painting

All Saints grand tower dwarfs the rest of the church

Tiny Tibenham to the south west of Long Stratton is easily overlooked, but the tall tower of All Saints is a beacon for miles around. Close to, it is seen to dwarf the rest of the church, which appears even more compressed due to the low clerestory. The tower is embellished with generous flushwork, particularly attractively on the base course and parapet. The symbols of the four Evangelists stand at the corners at the top and a bold stair turret ascends the south face. The rest of the church shows evidence of considerably older age than the C15th tower, especially in the north walls, where there is ancient herringbone coursing, probably Saxo-Norman, best shown in the nave wall but also present in the chancel wall, and a Norman slit window with deep splay. Internally, All Saints is fascinating, with some fine objects and exceptional features. In the period up to 1800 the prominent Norfolk family of Buxton exercised a strong influence over the church and it is reminders of their dynasty that, in part, characterise the interior. Chief amongst these is the looming bulk of the Buxton pew, an elevated seating area accessed via a staircase and constructed across the east end of the south aisle. There is little in the way of luxurious features in the pew, so it seems likely that it was provisioned for the servants and retainers of the family. On the side facing the nave is a Buxton coat of arms and on the side looking west into the aisle is a large hatchment. Brasses for Buxton family members are mounted on the walls near the pew, the clearest dating from 1572. The arcade is typical of the C14th, with quatrefoil piers and bell capitals. One of the grandest objects on view is the magnificent Jacobean pulpit, with its large, flamboyant tester. Nearby is a rather more formal C17th lectern, possibly later in date. The top opening to the rood survives. Part of the plangent, antique atmosphere of All Saints is due to the old roofs, the south aisle example is particularly notable and has delicate carving with shields in the spandrels. The chancel roof also boasts elegant carving in the spandrels. Many C19th 'improving texts' survive on the walls from a Victorian refurnishing, and earlier box pews are still in place. The chancel piscina and sedilia are fine examples, the latter with dividing arm rest, and old chests can be seen at the west end. A small medieval wall painting of a figure lurks beside the pulpit. The excellent C14th font has Decorated tracery on the bowl.

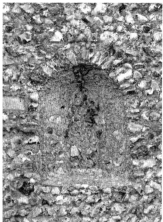

All Saints from the north east and south east

Norman window, north nave wall

Interior looking east

…. and west

The chancel

South aisle and Buxton pew

C19th banner & north doorway

Piscina and sedilia

Wall painting

The pulpit

Box pews and south aisle

From the Buxton pew

The font and arcade

179

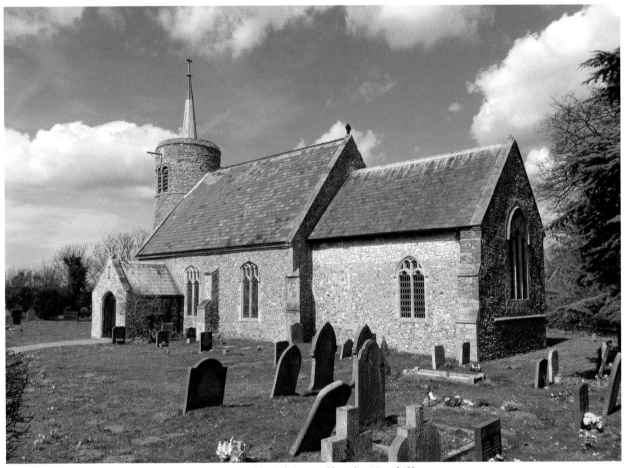

A 'Hertfordshire spike' in Norfolk

Titchwell is a name familiar to thousands of bird-watchers, who flock to the large coastal reserve here throughout the year, but just as attractive as many of the feathered denizens of Titchwell is the church of St Mary, with its ancient tower topped by a 'Hertfordshire spike'. This is a slim, lead-coated mini-spire that characterises many churches in that southern county, but which is very unusual in Norfolk. The tower on which it sits is an early one, usually assigned to the Norman period, but it has a feature that suggests older origins. There is little doubt that the larger belfry openings are Norman, they show typical Romanesque architecture, but there is a tiny window about halfway up the tower on the west side that has distinctive primitive features, especially the top which is formed of two large, rough pieces of flint set against each other to produce a pointed head. That type of configuration is often taken as a pre-Norman indicator. There are traces of Norman features elsewhere in the church. To either side of the tower the outline of the much narrower Norman nave can just be discerned, this was widened during an extensive C15th rebuilding. The chancel east wall now contains a Perpendicular-style window but enough has been left exposed of the earlier arrangement to ascertain that once two (probably three) semi-circular headed Norman windows were set here. Externally the blocked north doorway has a pointed arch, but inside its true Norman origins can be confirmed by the semi-circular arch. There are some nice Early English features too, particularly the fine south doorway (with stoup alongside), with its typical slim piers and moulded arch. Both nave doorways were reset at the time of the C15th rebuilding. An Early English piscina with ogee head can be seen in the chancel, originally this would have been a splendid example, but it was mutilated to accommodate the Perpendicular window and drop-sill sedilia which stand alongside. The plain tub font is also Norman, and like many others, it was banished for many years to serve as a drinking trough before being restored to its rightful place and set on a new stem. A font of very different type stands out of use in the sanctuary, this is a dainty C18th model. It was gifted from Burnham Deepdale when that church reinstated its marvellous Norman 'Labours of the months' font. Some of the C19th stained glass is good, especially The Sower of 1897 in the west window.

St Mary from the south west and north west

Very early window

Interior looking east

The sanctuary

Interior looking west

Tower arch

Font and blocked north doorway

C18[th] font

Mutilated piscina

West window ('The Sower') and nave window glass

The south doorway

From the south

The fine Grade 1 church of St Margaret lies in the deep countryside of south Norfolk, and enjoys a peaceful and evocative setting, a little way off from the main centre of its scattered parent village. About a mile away are the romantic ruins of the church of St Mary, damaged by a sonic boom in 1949 and never rehabilitated. St Margaret externally is unremarkable, except for the markedly different pitches of the roofs. It seems that the original steep pitch of the nave roof, set for thatch, was flattened to a lower level when rebuilt, while the chancel roof was left at its original pitch, despite losing its thatch. Much of the church is C14th, and mercifully, it escaped pervasive Victorian restoration. The C15th porch has settled over the years, resulting in the eccentric shape of the outer doorway. The assertive outline of the inner doorway is distinguished by a square head with spandrels enclosing shields. The interior is a delight and contains one of the finest objects in any Norfolk church, a quite exceptional wooden tympanum which stretches across the top half of the chancel arch. For any such feature to have survived is rare enough, but this one, in the main, is a magnificent royal arms of Elizabeth I of 1587. But that isn't all, the tympanum also carries the Ten Commandments, heraldic motifs associated with the family of Elizabeth, and other minor texts. All in all, it is a remarkable tour-de-force of national importance. The rest of the interior is perfectly in harmony with the tympanum, and contains many fascinating objects from days long past. Across the lower half of the chancel arch is a fine C15th or C16th screen, nobly patinated and given character by the passing years, and bearing delicate tracery, gilt-work, painted motifs and shields on the dado panels. The nave benches are most appealing, some are medieval and feature distinctive slim poppyheads with candle holders, and severely mutilated bench end figures. Others are later (but pre-Victorian) and of curious rustic design. The chancel has three intriguing openings, one is an individual Easter Sepulchre, of conservative design, with a tomb lid for a seat. There is also a thin niche beside the altar and a spindly piscina with an odd, bulbous finial. The C14th font is plain and undistinguished. Both rood openings survive, the lower one protected by a door. The church is almost devoid of stained glass, but the east window contains a few nondescript medieval fragments.

Views from the south east and north   South doorway

Looking north east across nave   The chancel   West from the sanctuary   West from the screen

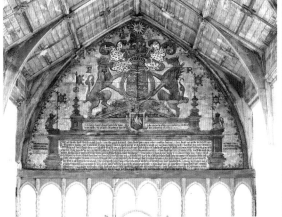

The fabulous tympanum   Rood openings, pulpit, screen   Screen dado

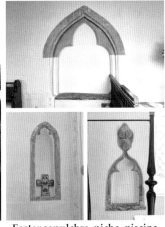

Benches   Medieval bench end   Easter sepulchre, niche, piscina   The font

A crisp February day at St Margaret

Toft Monks is one of many unusual Norfolk place names, the origins of which can give fascinating insights into the early settlement of the county. In this case 'Toft' is Old Scandinavian and means a homestead or farm, and the affix was added when monks from Préaux Abbey founded a religious centre here in the C11th. Presumably the monks built the first church here, and Norman features can still be seen in the building today. The exotic octagonal tower as seen from the outside is not Norman, but is probably not much later, the distinctive lancet windows and lovely array of tall lancet belfry openings are an Early English indicator. But features on the internal west wall, consisting of the tower arch (later the head was made pointed), two deeply splayed windows, a round-headed door with, to the right, a large round-headed niche and above, another doorway, are all unmistakeably Norman. Thus, it could be concluded that the present octagonal tower was built around an earlier Norman one, or a Norman one collapsed and was rebuilt in its present form in Early English times, but with the internal west wall Norman details being retained. Exactly what function some of these openings had is unclear. The chancel is also Early English, and has two open and two blocked lancets each side. The C15th porch has neat flushwork externally, and, inside, an impressive roof with curiously weathered corbels, weirdly pale and ghostly. The interior has a piquant, ancient feel despite some Victorian refitting, and good things reside here. The C15th font has been attacked by both iconoclasts and green algae but isn't in bad shape; the design is commonplace, with Evangelist's symbols and angels on the bowl, and lions around the stem. The cover is an admirable example from the C17th. There are two royal arms, both fairly uncommon. One of 1661 for Charles II on the north wall is in a parlous state, but the other above the south door for George II is in better condition. In the chancel are the church's only two significant wall memorials, one appears to be an amalgam of various pieces salvaged from a chest tomb of 1653, for John Bayspoole, while the other is a moderately ornate wall tablet for two members of the Lodington family, of 1789. Across from the memorials is a rather plain piscina. Two inscription brasses date from 1607 and 1610. The east window glass is a stern Christ of 1952 designed by Thomas Derrick.

St Margaret from the south and north west

The south porch

Interior looking east

The sanctuary

Looking west from the sanctuary

Nave roof

George II royal arms

Glass by Thomas Derrick

The font

Two inscription brasses 1607 and 1610

Remnants of Bayspoole tomb

Lodington tablet 1789

Porch corbel

St Margaret bathed in winter sunshine

Oddly, the alphabetical structure of this book has thrown up two St Margarets in a row, both with very rare octagonal towers, although Topcroft St Margaret is only octagonal in its topmost three quarters. The lowest stage is round, and it seems that the rest of an original Norman round tower collapsed or became delapidated fairly early on in its life, necessitating a rebuilding in the C13th. Perhaps the builder who rebuilt the tower thought an octagonal shape was more attractive. There was another intervention in the C15th, when the top stage and battlements were rebuilt. By then, octagonal belfry stages were popular. The internal tower arch is not, as might be expected, Norman, but is a later replacement, acutely pointed. The chancel was completely rebuilt in 1712 in the then fashionable and easily constructed material of brick. It boasts thin pilasters, but the Decorated-style windows are C19th replacements. By the C18th piscinas and sedilia had passed out of fashion and use, and there are none in the chancel here. However, the aisle has a rather nice medieval one at the east end, confirming that a chapel was once established there. The font is a very familiar C15th type, with angels and lions with lively tails around the bowl and somewhat mutilated lions supporting the stem. The arcade with its short piers is C14th, but these have earlier bases. Both rood openings are extant, note the very low setting for the upper doorway, indicating that the loft must also have been at no great height above the floor. The royal arms is Hanoverian but to which George it is dedicated is not clear, as there are only the letters GR, without numbers, as in George I, but the arms are dated 1789, when George III was on the throne. A feature of the chancel are the numerous and varied C18th and C19th wall memorials, for families such as local bigwigs, the Smyths. But one of the best is mounted to the right of the south chancel arch pier, facing into the nave. It is for Richard Wilton, who died in 1637, and the text is in Latin. See also a matching pair of long, oval tablets for James and John Smyth, the first from the late years of the C18th and the second from the early years of the C19th. Refurbishment by the Victorians included one of their favourite enthusiasms, stencilling, which was later largely eradicated from our churches, but here parts of a large scheme remain, with floral decoration and biblical texts on banners.

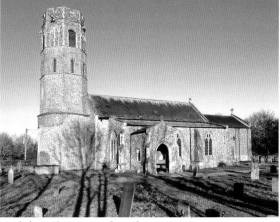

The church from the west and south west

Chancel commemoration stone

The interior looking east and west

Font, tower arch, stencilling

The font

Rood openings & pulpit

Arcade stencilling

Aisle piscina

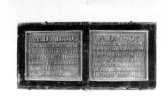

Benefaction boards

Chancel wall tablets

Wilton tablet, 1637

Hanoverian royal arms/Hatchment

187

Large and splendid, St Mary from the south

It is difficult to avoid overuse of the word 'atmospheric' when discussing the churches of the deep Norfolk countryside, especially those, like St Mary, that stand isolated and adrift from their nominal settlements. Here the use is unavoidable, no other word gives the sense of otherness that characterises these places. That feeling is even more acute here, because St Mary is such an imposing church, with aisles and a south porch added to the impressive nave and chancel. More impact is given by the unusual clerestory, which features blind flushwork arcading instead of windows, of different designs north and south. And then there is the style of the building, built as it was during the transitional years between the Decorated and Perpendicular periods. Compare the reticulated windows of the nave with the Perpendicular ones of the chancel, for instance. It is likely that only a few decades separate them. Inside, the feeling of being inside a time capsule is unavoidable, as a whiff of the middle ages is quite palpable, especially in the chancel where a most uncommon sight greets the visitor. That is a small, narrow room built against the east wall, which has a platform on the top, steps to the north and small doorway to the south. Two small battered niches are set in the wall, with two large ones in the east wall proper. A common suggestion is that the building served as a reliquary and the platform was for showing them off, but the idea of it being a sacristy also has credibility. A short walk to the west reveals another grand medieval object, the C15th rood screen. This is in very good order and also retains the platform and some of the framework of the original loft. The dado has 16 portraits of the Apostles and the Latin Doctors, in authentic medieval condition, their faces damaged by iconoclasts. The striking chancel piscina and sedilia set are in excellent condition thanks to a restoration in recent years. As is the admirable Victorian font at the west end. Two other piscinas in the aisles, more or less identical, are undoubtedly medieval. There are medieval features elsewhere, like the springer heads on the C14th arcades and a plinth for a statue, with angel underneath. Two Victorian wall tablets for members of the Mack family are worth finding, as is an old poor box. Don't leave St Mary without seeing the intricate medieval metalwork on the south door.

West doorway

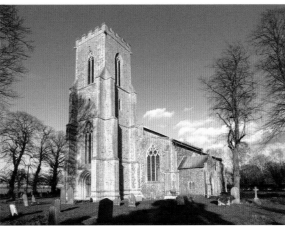

St Mary from the south west

South doorway medieval metalwork

Interior looking west

The chancel

Interior and screen

Screen north and south

St Philip

Steps to the east end platform

Chancel piscina and sedilia

North & south aisle piscinas/plinth

The font

Mack tablet, mid-C19th

Poor box

189

WELLINGHAM ST ANDREW

A classic country church, St Andrew at Wellingham

A perfectly charming building in a charming setting, St Andrew is a gem amongst Norfolk's smaller churches. Not for its magnificent architecture or grand survivals, with one glorious exception, but for that elusive sense of romance that emanates from an ancient English church in a tiny, unspoilt village. It is also that rare beast, a church that can be viewed without impediment from all points of the churchyard, with no intrusive trees, bushes, high walls or fences to obscure the prospect. That being so, it can be appreciated that despite a big Victorian renovation scheme, the remaining lancet windows indicate that the church is basically C13th, with later windows inserted in the C14th and C15th. There are no aisles, although at first it might be thought that the curious arcade in the south wall (only seen inside) might be left from a demolished one. However, it appears to be simply decorative, there are no piers. The tower with its stepped parapet is quite plain otherwise, without buttresses, but it looks a little odd because the top stage is narrower than the bottom. Large pieces of dressed limestone in the tower's fabric, especially in the north and west faces, are intriguing and probably recycled. Inside, the lack of frequent use is reflected in the need for some repair and maintenance, and there are few items of significance. But one of Norfolk's most enthralling rood screens has, in part, survived the passing of the centuries since installation in 1532. Only the dado remains, with three big panels each side. Two have lost their paintings, but the four that retain them are of great interest and rarity. For most of these are not mere portraits, but animated scenes, like stills from a film, and some depict very unusual subjects. From north to south are St Sebastian, bristling with arrows, sharing a panel with a mysterious figure (more on him later), followed by St George dispatching his dragon to an appreciative audience, St Michael weighing souls and finally, an extraordinary Resurrection full of symbolic iconography. The mystery man, with Tudor cap, ermine stole, and sword and spear may be St Maurice, a martyr, and here he stands on the fallen figure of his nemesis, Emperor Diocletian. Maurice is very rarely seen in Norfolk, and, intriguingly, he is usually portrayed abroad as a black man. Little else demands attention, but see the plain old font, simple piscina and drop-sill sedilia and a small wall tablet of 1637 near the pulpit.

St Andrew from the west and north east   South doorway

The interior looking east and west   Piscina and sedilia

Around the pulpit   Ss Sebastian & ?Maurice   St George   St Michael and the Resurrection

Becke tablet, 1637   Morecraft ledger slab, C18th   The font   Chancel piscina

WEREHAM ST MARGARET of ANTIOCH

B3, TF 681 017

St Margaret from the north

Wereham is a medium-sized village a few miles east of Downham Market in the west of Norfolk. Once off the busy A134 the true nature of this super place becomes apparent. A walk or drive along Church Street reveals many lovely cottages and a strong sense of continuity with the past, and when the village pond and St Margaret's church are reached visitors find themselves in the midst of a classic picture postcard scene, with fine buildings ringing the ancient pond. Here are the old school, the traditional village pub and many other attractive vistas. And of course the church, beautifully set. The surprising thing is that Wereham is, like its church, little visited. St Margaret is a curious church with a quite different feel to most others in Norfolk. It retains parts and hints of many building campaigns, overprinted very strongly by a pervasive restoration of 1866, which followed a fire; unravelling the story of the evolution of the building is not straightforward. Nave, chancel and tower are from the late 1200's, with the south aisle from the early 1300's, judging by the arcade. The north aisle and its arcade were constructed in 1866, to replicate the southern one. The tower fabric is fascinating, although the whole church repays the attentions of the building stone enthusiast. In the tower many different stones can be identified, including large and small irregular pieces of ferrous conglomerate, several courses of which can be seen towards the top. Also dressed blocks of what appears to be Silver Carr, which is also used in the buttresses, plus brown Carstone, brick, flint and quartzite pebbles. Two long thin lancets and the west doorway confirm a C13th assignment. The brick parapet is C16th. A prominent sundial of 1725 adorns the south face. The tower arch internally is interesting, because above the small C13th opening are the remnants of an earlier, much larger arch, suggesting that the tower was rebuilt from a ?Norman original, perhaps round. The 1866 restoration dominates the interior, but there are a number of moderate-good wall tablets and memorials, particularly from the late C18th. The deeply-splayed east wall lancets of the chancel are arranged in the classic Early English three-form and, though restored, are original, with framing of chalk clunch. The font is a dull, plain C14th example, while the cut-down royal arms are Hanoverian. The Victorian stone pulpit is distinctive. The village bier stands ready for use.

The church from the west and south

The tower & sundial from the south

Interior looking east

The chancel

The nave from the east

South aisle from the east

Adamson, Heaton & Adamson (II) tablets

Houchen wall tablet, 1832

C18th & C19th tablets

Hanoverian royal arms

The font

The pulpit

Parish bier

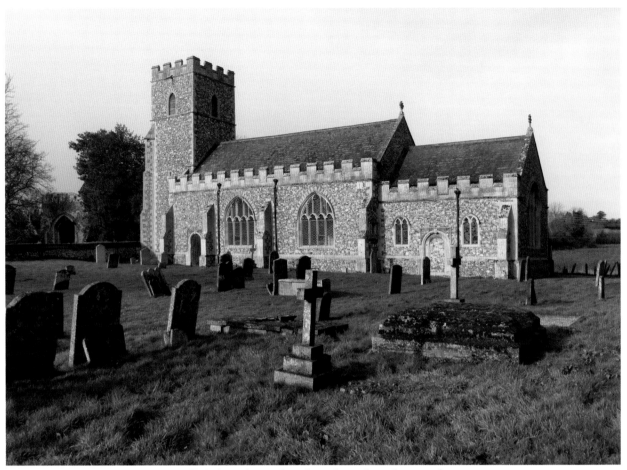

All Saints from the churchyard to the south

At first glance All Saints looks like a standard, modest medieval church, attractively set in a quiet country hamlet. But there is much more to the church than just those bare facts. To begin it stands very near to the evocative ruins of the C12[th] Augustinian priory of St Mary and All Saints. The priory had its own church, but some association between the two churches may reasonably be assumed before 1538, when the priory was dissolved by Henry VIII. The fine gatehouse of the priory is situated just to the west of All Saints. The decaying church was extensively reconfigured c.1638 in the Perpendicular style using stone from the ruined priory to create a rough chequerboard effect. 1638 was a very unusual time for church building, right at the last gasp of that period. However, both north porch, south and chancel doorways have Classical stylings. The chancel arch and tower are C14[th], but the windows of the latter were renewed in the C17[th]. The tower clock of 1907 exhorts us to 'watch and pray'. Local magnate Sir Edward Barkham, whose arms appear at several points around the exterior, was responsible for the C17[th] rebuilding. Standing out are the assertive battlements which run all around the church, the considerable northern vestry and details around the north porch, including a death's head keystone in the outer doorway and an eroded, C13[th] carving of a seated figure by the inner doorway. These may have come from the priory. The interior feels spacious, due to the wide nave and large chancel arch, but there are no aisles. Little was retained from the early church at the time of the rebuilding. The small, unadorned font was perhaps installed new as part of the 1638 restoration. The royal arms is for George III, but it is a little difficult to see because of reflections from the nearby window. A hatchment of 1824 for Philip Hamond is set above the north doorway. Many splendid memorials to members of the Hamond family beautify the chancel, particularly outstanding are two commanding examples featuring a languid, mourning lady and a graceful angel, for Frances of 1820 and Anthony of 1822. Hamonds are also commemorated in the chancel stained glass. The east window of 1907 by Burlison & Grylls remembers four brothers, their representations and the biblical scenes are quite exquisite. The striking altar rails are C17[th]. Intriguing old wooden carvings are set into the reredos and altar front.

Tower and clock from the north

All Saints from the north east

Death's head, north porch outer doorway

Interior from the west

All Saints east end

Interior from the east

Font and tower arch

For Anthony and Frances Hamond

Browne tablet, C18th

Panels from the east window

George III royal arms

Painted roundel

Hamond hatchment, 1824

195

WESTON LONGVILLE ALL SAINTS

All Saints from the south west

All Saints is a lucky church, it will never want for visitors. In fact, there is almost a beaten trail to its door, all due to the enthusiasm of one man for keeping a diary. The Rev'd James Woodforde, or Parson Woodforde as he is better known, was rector of Weston Longville from 1773 to his death in 1803, and for almost all that time he kept a detailed diary of the goings on in his own life and that of his parish, minor and major. As well as giving a strong and heady taste of life in the later years of the C18th, it is the everyday events that are so appealing, the sheer humanity of his writings that so engage the reader. The diaries also cover his life before he came to Weston. Woodforde 'fans', for the diaries were first published, in part, in the 1920's and proved immensely popular, are regular visitors to All Saints. And a fine, cherished church awaits them, worthy of anyone's attention. The low tower is C13th and has stood the test of time very well, while the rest of the church is mostly C14th and C15th, with thorough restoration undertaken in the C19th. There are two aisles and a C15th south porch, with flushwork and niche above its outer doorway. There is a great deal to see inside. The font at the west end is plain and of little interest, but set into the lower west step is a remnant from an ancient cross, said to be Saxon, showing very faintly the crucified Christ. On the west wall nearby are a George III royal arms in good restored condition and a painting of Parson Woodforde by his nephew. Several wall paintings have been uncovered in fairly recent times, the ones of John the Baptist (next to the chancel arch) and a large Tree of Jesse (north wall) are the best. The C15th rood screen is amongst the best in Norfolk and features excellent Perpendicular tracery and a dado with 12 paintings of the Apostles, all named, each holding a line from the Creed. The paintings are vivid and clear, thanks to successive restorations, which fortunately have not spoiled them. Near the screen is a brass of 1533 for Elizabeth Rokewood, seen with her two children. There is also a simple inscription brass. The piscina and sedilia set in the chancel is excellent, with ornament in part of green men. Both rood openings, and stairs, are still in place. There is decent old glass in south aisle windows, made up with much later work. Some box pews survive and there are a few good wall tablets, including an elegant one for Parson Woodforde. The C19th altar reredos is restrained and tasteful.

Tower and porch

From the north west and east

Interior from the west

The chancel

Nave from the east

Rood screen

Screen, north side

Piscina and sedilia

South east corner, nave

The Tree of Jesse

The font

Rokewood brass, 1533

Norwich School angel

Parson Woodforde tablet, 1803

WICKHAMPTON ST ANDREW E3, TG 427 055

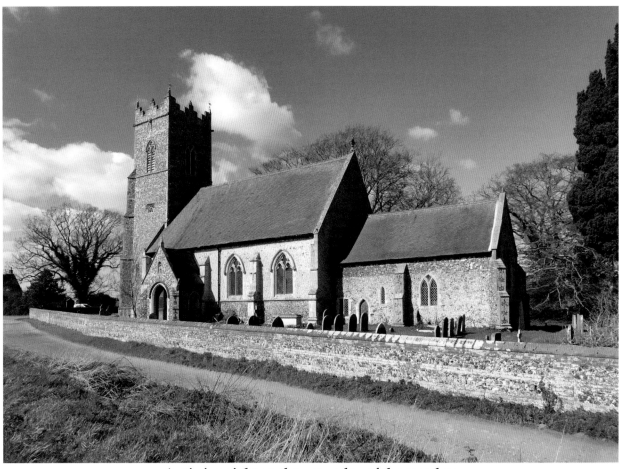

A stirring sight on the very edge of the marshes

Wickhampton St Andrew stands on the very brink of wide marshes through which the Yare, The Fleet and the Waveney lazily meander. Once that area was a large tidal estuary. Beyond to the east is the sprawl of Great Yarmouth, Norfolk's second largest settlement. The wetlands are not the wild, untamed wilderness they once were, but on a day of freezing fog in deepest winter the atmosphere positively tingles on the lonely walk into the flatlands from the church to Berney Arms and its isolated station. One can imagine the relief of people who worked in the marshes in the days before electricity and the internal combustion engine when they reached the church on their way home on a day of bad weather. St Andrew matches well its surroundings and it is an ancient church redolent with the haunting music of the past. Many reminders of those far off days still exist here, as we shall see inside. The building externally has evidence of at least C13th origins, there are two lancet windows (with Norman-type inner splays) in the chancel to confirm that. To the south is a slightly later Y-traceried window and an archetypal low-side window. The rest is largely C14th, the nave early in that century and the tower towards the end. The handsome tower has nice flushwork in the base course, a west doorway, delicately-traceried sound holes, stepped battlements and weathervanes on its figure-pinnacles. The restored porch retains a niche above the outer doorway, now housing a modern statue of St Andrew. The first of many fine things inside attracts the eye immediately. This is a series of large C14th wall paintings on the nave north wall, discovered in the C19th. From west to east the major scenes are the allegory The Three Living and the Three Dead, St Christopher, and a very rare depiction of the Seven Works of Mercy with an additional panel showing the Resurrection. All are in remarkable order. Two exceptional and well-preserved C13th tombs reside in the chancel, with effigies of Sir William Gerbygge and his wife, lying on low chests and surrounded by exquisite canopies. Sir William holds his heart. Two C15th inscription brasses are wall mounted on wooden boards. The George III royal arms is almost illegible. The pulpit is a dignified C17th example and the font apparently modern. There is an old chest and a wall-mounted medieval bench end, which was copied for the modern bench ends.

198

St Andrew from the west and south west

The porch

Looking north east across the church

The sanctuary

Interior looking west

3 Living and 3 Dead/7 Works of Mercy

St Christopher

Sir William and Lady Gerbygge

C15th brasses

The pulpit

The font

George III royal arms

Chest, bench end, head

199

Holy Trinity and All Saints from Black Street

Many centuries ago the sea was closer to Holy Trinity, and its magnificent tower, all of 40m (130′) of it, would have efficiently fulfilled its secondary function as a beacon to mariners. Even today, after the expansion seaward of an ecologically important expanse of dunes has pushed Holy Trinity further inland, it can still be clearly seen from the water. The C15th tower is a marvellous construction and boasts fancy buttresses with flushwork and more fine flushwork in two contrasting patterns around the base course. The topmost stage is full of stylistic flourishes, including stepped, panelled and ornamented battlements, a corbel table mostly of heads, flushwork, gargoyles and statues. The rest of the church cowers beneath all that majesty but has its own merits. Both nave and chancel have C19th battlements, and the nave is very wide and spacious. Perhaps there were once aisles, now absorbed into the nave. The C15th porch has a fine, ornate façade, sadly much reduced by weather and salty air. The Victorians had a big say in how the church looks today, and the restoration of diocesan architect Herbert Green in the late 1870′s will never be universally admired. However, a fire in the C17th may have decimated the medieval fittings, and before the overhaul in the C19th, the church was in a very poor state, so it appears that restoration was essential. Apparently unrestored was the odd lean-to vestry built off the chancel north wall, whose lancet windows are C13th. On entering, the lofty and wide nave comes as a bit of a surprise, but it is soon apparent that the interior is rather unusually furnished. In keeping with Winterton's maritime past there is a 'fisherman's corner' with nets and other seafaring odds and ends, including tablets and plaques remembering brave deeds. One records the valiant attempt of Rev'd Porter in 1932 to rescue a choirboy. He drowned, but the choirboy was saved. Either side of the chancel arch are two similar altars, with matching tablets above. Two C14th piscinas, one in the chancel and one in the nave, confirm at least that date for the fabric of the church. The chancel example is eroded, but quite impressive. An important treasure and usually overlooked because of its high position above the tall chancel arch is a royal arms for Charles I. Nearly all the fittings are C19th, but of good quality, especially the pulpit, screen and altar rails. The wall tablets are respectable, but not of the first rank.

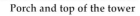

Porch and top of the tower

Holy Trinity from the north

Tower flushwork

Interior looking south east

The chancel

West from the screen

East from the nave

Nave north east

The font

Chancel piscina

Wall tablets, Porter memorial and Husband brass of 1676

Charles I royal arms

Let there be light

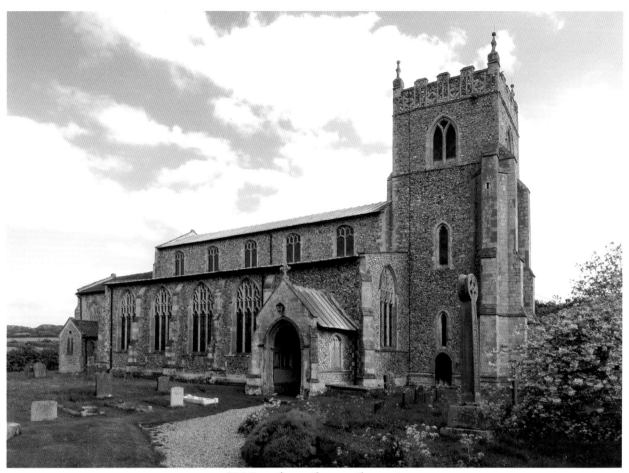

St Mary from the north west

St Mary enjoys a beautiful position, overlooking the silted up vestiges of a once important harbour to the east and a pleasant green to the west. Beyond the harbour lies the much-celebrated Cley church, completing a superb panorama. St Mary is every bit as good as its surroundings, and is a rewarding alternative to busy Cley in the tourist season. It has a full set of elements in its layout, of west tower with C17th baroque pinnacles, aisled nave with fine porches to the north and south, chancel and north sacristy. The tower, sacristy and chancel are the earliest parts, of early C14th age (although the intersecting east window and its internal slim shafts might indicate an earlier Early English foundation). The chancel in part is adorned with very early flushwork. All the other parts of the church including the clerestory are C15th and possess impressive, matching Perpendicular windows, the design of which echoes earlier Decorated forms. Put aside plenty of time inside, there is much to see. The early C14th font is damaged, it seems that bowl panel carvings and the angels beneath were obliterated during a period of iconoclasm. The stately arcades soar high and the chancel and tower arches are similarly tall. Above the arches of the arcades facing the nave are black letter biblical texts in good order, which may be Victorian or somewhat earlier. Above the chancel arch is a large window which previously lit the rood. The stairs to the rood remain to the north side of the arch, but are concealed behind, unusually, two doorways, the one in the chancel blocked whilst the other in the north aisle has a door. A nice set of box pews of 1849 fills the nave and aisles. The tower arch screen was probably the original rood screen, cut-down to fill its new position and painted a drab brown, beneath which lie, possibly, much more interesting original paintings. The aisle windows are cut down to provide seating. Four excellent C15th and C16th brasses exist here, all have figures, including a rare shroud brass complete with skeletal figure. A rather naively painted George III post-1816 royal arms is mounted above the chancel arch. In the chancel are an unremarkable piscina and drop-sill sedilia. A few old benches with poppyheads survive. A lovely fragment of C15th glass recently discovered behind masonry is now mounted for display. The early C16th Greneway Charity Box is an outstanding item. The church was restored in 1863 by Thomas Jeckyll.

The church from the west and south east

Chancel east wall, with flushwork

Interior looking east

The chancel

Interior looking west

Piscina and sedilia

Tower screen

Old benches

George III arms/Greneway Charity Box

C15th glass

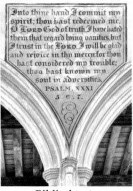

George and Ann Brigge, William Bisshop, Thomas Brigge brasses

Biblical text

The font

203

Sunshine bathes St Peter's mellow carstone

At one point in the late 1800's St Peter was almost derelict, but then an unexpected saviour arrived, in the shape of the heir to the British throne Prince Edward, who decided to build his new country pied-a-terre at Sandringham in 1870. The enthusiastic Prince was soon casting his eye over the rest of the neighbourhood and was clearly not pleased with the state of the local churches, and set about smartening them up. He gave the work at Wolferton to a trusted architect, Sir Arthur Blomfield, and he undertook a sober, but thorough, restoration, filling St Peter with sound and serious furniture. He turned out most of the interior fittings but, thankfully, left enough medieval material to interest church historians. St Peter's building material, the locally outcropping Carstone of Cretaceous age, is not always suitable for building, but when sufficiently durable it gives rise to most attractive buildings of a variable brown hue, as here. Limestone, probably from the East Midlands, was used for the facings, door and window surrounds, and tracery. The barn-like interior appears sparsely filled, but it soon becomes apparent that there is more here than initially thought, and the church contains an intriguing mixture of features and fittings from the middle ages to recent times. The medieval is represented by the font, screen dado, parclose chapel screens, piscinas and sedilia, tiles, stone coffins, rood stair doorways and lower elements of the nave roof. The basic fabric, which includes two fine C14th arcades with heads at the springing of the arches, and the tower and chancel arches, is C13th–C14th. The reddening of the arcades and other fabric is evidence of a big fire in 1486. Post-medieval features include the seating, stone pulpit, altars and rails, lectern (given by Princess Alexandra), chancel roof and most of the nave roof (all C19th), plus a superb C17th Italian lectern and an outstanding Elizabethan table in the north chapel. Of the important older items, the big font with traceried bowl, two piscinas and sedilia are probably C14th, the chancel screen dado is C15th and has vestiges of paintings, the intricately worked south parclose is C14th whilst the north is C15th and less ornate. The medieval section of the nave roof features wooden figures on the wall posts and figures holding shields above. The C19th Christ-in-Majesty painting above the chancel arch overlies a much older version. There are many more worthy things to discover here.

West doorway and window

St Peter from the north east

In the porch

Font and interior looking east

Chancel screen

Screen south side

Interior looking west

Parclose screens

Rood doorways, screens, pulpit

The north chapel

Chancel piscina and sedilia

Chancel arch painting

Nave roof wall post figures

Local characters

205

The village pond makes a pretty foreground to St Andrew

Wood Dalling lies in a sparsely populated area of scattered villages in central Norfolk. The intensely rural landscape hereabouts and the ancient winding roads give rise to a secretive atmosphere where the past feels very close, despite the land being largely given over to modern arable farming. It is therefore curious that near to St Andrew are some significantly large and heavy duty churches, such as the famous giants of Salle, Heydon and Cawston. To these can be added Wood Dalling. Admittedly, St Andrew is nowhere near as important or celebrated as the first three, but it is nonetheless a large and imposing pile, with an impressive tower, two aisles, two porches (the south with parvise and a doorway to it 2m above the ground inside) and C15th clerestory. There is good evidence of C13th origins in the chancel with its three lancet windows on the north side, and in the nave where there are C13th east responds to the arcades. A C15th campaign resulted in the insertion of stylish, matching Perpendicular windows in the aisles. The east and south east chancel windows are good, flowing C14th Decorated. The other Decorated-style window in the south chancel wall may be a C19th replacement and it partially obscures a brick arch, which possibly once led to a vanished chapel. The small south chancel priest's doorway is also blocked. The voluminous interior is stark and bare, an effect reinforced by the largely empty walls and skeletal old benches with their smart poppyheads. At first glance it appears that there is little worth consideration, but the longer the visitor persists, the more becomes apparent. For example, the many floor brasses here could easily be missed, there are a surprising number, although none are of the best quality or preservation, and several are inscription only. Some are for members of the local Bulwer dynasty and the age range is C15th to C17th, the older ones in Latin. An interesting insight into the attitude to these brasses by later occupants of the church is that arguably the best example in the church has a bench mounted right across it, and another is partially concealed beneath the pulpit. There is a nice ancient angle piscina in the chancel associated with drop-sill sedilia and the roofs are C15th or C16th; there are distinctive bosses in the nave. The font is a regulation Victorian example but the best thing inside is a medieval effigy of a priest in very good restored order.

St Andrew from the south west and south east   West doorway

North east across the church   The chancel   Interior looking west   Angle piscina and sedilia

Steps to the parvise   The font   Effigy of a priest   Bulwer tablet (1815)

Figure and inscription brasses   Nave seating/old poppyheads   Nave roof bosses

207

References and Select Bibliography

In essence, the references and bibliography entries here are a repeat of the same section in my first book of 100 Norfolk Churches, with the important exception of the Norfolk Church Guides part, which now consists of references to the churches in this book. A small websites section has also been added. Readers are referred to the first book for commentary on, and evaluation of, certain of the various titles listed below, and for other discussion and information that will not be repeated here. However, as a starting point for any collection, the books by Cautley (1949), Mortlock and Roberts (2007) and Pevsner and Wilson (1997, 1999) are essential. Excellent recent additions to the catalogue of books concerning Norfolk churches are by Page and Young (2014), and three books by Tolhurst (2014, 2015, 2016).

Norfolk Churches

Cautley, H.M. 1949. Norfolk Churches. Norman Adlard & Co. Ltd., Ipswich.

Chadwick, O. 1983. Victorian Miniature. Futura Macdonald & Co., London.

Fawcett, R. 1974. The Architecture and Furnishings of Norfolk Churches. The Norfolk Society.

Goode, W.J. 1994. Round Tower Churches of south east England. Round Towers Churches Society.

Greenwood, R. and Norris, M. 1976. The Brasses of Norfolk Churches. Norfolk Churches Trust.

Harrod, W. 1972. Norfolk Country Churches and the Future. The Norfolk Society.

Harrod, W. and Linnell, C.L.S. 1969. Shell Guide to Norfolk. Faber & Faber Ltd., London.

Hart, S. 2003. The Round Tower Churches of England. Lucas Books.

Jeffrey, P.H. 1989. God's East Anglia. The Old Orchard Press, Gillingham, Norfolk.

King, D.J. 1974. Stained Glass Tours around Norfolk Churches. The Norfolk Society.

Marr, L. 1979. From my Point of View. A personal record of some Norfolk Churches. Acorn Editions, Fakenham.

Mee, A. 1959. The King's England, Norfolk. Hodder & Stoughton, London.

Mortlock, D.P. and Roberts, C.V. 2007. The Guide to Norfolk Churches. The Lutterworth Press, Cambridge.

Page, M. and Young P. 2014. Norfolk Churches from the Air. Poppyland Publishing, Cromer.

Pevsner, N. 1962. The Buildings of England. Norfolk. Vol. 1, North-east Norfolk and Norwich. Vol. 2, North-west and South Norfolk. Penguin Books.

Pevsner, N. and Wilson, B. 1997. The Buildings of England. Norfolk 1: Norwich and North-East (2nd new edition). Yale University Press.

Pevsner, N. and Wilson, B. 1999. The Buildings of England. Norfolk 2: North-West and South (2nd new edition). Yale University Press.

Pye, A.S. 2010. A photographic and historical guide to the Parish Churches of Central Norfolk, including a guide to architectural styles, saints and pulpits. ASPYE, Lowestoft.

Pye, A.S. 2010. A photographic and historical guide to the Parish Churches of West Norfolk, including a guide to fonts and parish chests. ASPYE, Lowestoft.

Pye, A.S. 2010. A photographic and historical guide to the Parish Churches of East Norfolk, including a guide to royal arms. ASPYE, Lowestoft.

Shreeve, D. and Stilgoe, E. 2001. The Round Tower Churches of Norfolk. Canterbury Press, Norwich.

Spencer, N. 1977. Sculptured Monuments in Norfolk Churches. The Norfolk Churches Trust, Norwich.

Stanford, D. 2007. Norfolk Churches. Frances Lincoln, London.

Sterry, J. 2003. Round Tower Churches. Hidden Treasures of North Norfolk. Jack Sterry, Kenilworth.

Sterry, J. 2005. Round Tower Churches on the Norfolk and Suffolk Border. Jack Sterry, Kenilworth.

Sterry, J. 2007. Round Tower Churches to the West, East and South of Norwich. Jack Sterry, Kenilworth.

Sterry, J. 2010. Round Tower Churches in Mid Norfolk, North Norfolk and Suffolk. Jack Sterry, Kenilworth.

Swift, A. 2015. 100 Norfolk Churches of Village and Countryside. Velox Books, Leicester.

The Norfolk Churches Trust. 2001. Treasure for the future. A Celebration. The Norfolk Churches Trust, Norwich.

Tilbrook, R. and Roberts, C.V. 1997. Norfolk's Churches: Great and Small. Jarrold Publishing, Norwich.

Tolhurst, P. 2014. Norfolk Parish Treasures: North and West Norfolk. Black Dog Books, Norwich.

Tolhurst, P. 2015. Norfolk Parish Treasures: Breckland and South Norfolk. Black Dog Books, Norwich.

Tolhurst, P. 2016. Norfolk Parish Treasures: Mid Norfolk and The Broads. Black Dog Books, Norwich.

Wallace, D. and Bagnall Oakeley, R.P. 1951. The County Books. Norfolk. Robert Hale Ltd., London.

Norfolk Church Guides

Normally to be found in churches, these are either single or multiple sheets, folded or unfolded, or stapled small booklets. They vary enormously in quality, amount of information and availability. The guides listed below are the ones obtained from the named churches. Where a church is not listed, there was no guide available at the time of visits. That does not imply that one or more doesn't exist. There are an increasing number of guides to be found online, on individual church or benefice websites. Again, the information given is very variable.

Antingham. Anon. 2012. The Churches of Antingham. Revised edition.

Antingham. Anon. N.D. Churches in the Repps Deanery Welcome You. Poppyland Partnership.

Ashby St Mary. Anon. N.D. The Church of St Mary the Virgin, Ashby St Mary.

Bintree. Anon. N.D. Church of St. Swithun Bintree (Bintry).

Blofield. Grainger, E.R. 2012. The Parish church of St. Andrew and St. Peter, Blofield, Norfolk. Historical Guide.

Blofield. Anon. N.D. Welcome to the Church of St Andrew & St Peter, Blofield.

Bodham. Anon. N.D. Holt Deanery Church Trail, Diocese of Norwich. 6. Bodham All Saints.

Bodham. The Weybourne Group of Parishes. N.D. The Weybourne Group of Parishes on the North Norfolk Coast in the Diocese of Norwich.

Breccles. Cotton, S. N.D. Saint Margaret's Church, Breccles (or Breckles). Church Tours, Burwood Hall. Drawings by Holbeach, H.

Breckland. Anon. N.D. Churches One. Churches in the Wissey Valley. Breckland, the Secret Heart of Norfolk. Breckland Council, Norfolk.

Bridgham. Handley, J. & O'Neale, D. N.D. St. Mary the Virgin, Bridgham. Church Tours, Burwood Hall.

Broadland Churches. Bishop of Norwich. 1975. Some Broadland Churches. Jarrold and Sons Ltd., Norwich.

Burnham Sutton cum Ulph. Stilgoe, L. 2001. All Saints Church, Burnham Sutton cum Ulph. Church Tours, Burwood Hall. Drawings by Holbeach, H.

Burnham Sutton cum Ulph. Stilgoe, L. 2008. All Saints Church, Burnham Sutton cum Ulph. Church Tours, Burwood Hall. Revised edition. Drawings by Holbeach, H.

Castle Rising. Anon. N.D. Castle Rising Church.

Denver. Anon. N.D. St. Mary's Church, Denver.

Dickleburgh. Pierssene, A. and Trigwell, S. 1998. The Church of All Saints, Dickleburgh.

Dunton. Stapleford, R. 2011. St Peter's Dunton in Outstanding features of the Upper Wensum Churches.

East Winch. Steele, N. 2016. A Guide to All Saints Church, East Winch.

East Winch. Stilgoe, L. 2015. East Winch All Saints. Church Tours, Burwood Hall.

East Wretham. Kitson, J. 2010. St Ethelbert East Wretham. A Guide including the writings of the Rector, the Reverend James Park Whalley, at its rebuilding (1864-5).

Easton. Anon. N.D. Easton St. Peter's.

Elsing. Atkinson, H. N.D. Parish Church of Saint Mary the Virgin Elsing. Church Guide. Elsing Parochial Church Council.

Feltwell. Shapland, T. 2016. A Guide to St Mary's Church, Feltwell.

Field Dalling. Anon. N.D. Holt Deanery Church Trail, Diocese of Norwich. 13. Field Dalling St Andrew.

Field Dalling. Anon. N.D. St. Andrew's Church, Field Dalling. Church Tours, Burwood Hall.

Field Dalling. Hungate Medieval Art. N.D. Hungate Stained Glass Trails: No. 1 Stody, Bale, Field Dalling, Cley.

Fleggburgh. Anon. N.D. The South Trinity Broads Benefice Cycle Trail.

Flitcham. Butler-Stoney, R. 1985. The Church of St Mary, Flitcham. Church Tours, Burwood Hall. Drawings by Holbeach, H.

Flitcham. Stilgoe, L. 2013. Flitcham St Mary. Church Tours, Burwood Hall.

Fring. Stilgoe, L. 2013. Fring All Saints. Church Tours, Burwood Hall.

Garboldisham. Anon. N.D. The Churches of St John the Baptist and All Saints' Garboldisham, Norfolk.

Gateley. Stapleford, R. 2011. St Bart's Brisley *in* Outstanding features of the Upper Wensum Churches.

Gateley. Stilgoe, L. 2005. Gateley St Helen. Church Tours, Burwood Hall.

Great Ryburgh. Stapleford, R. 2011. St Andrew's Great Ryburgh *in* Outstanding features of the Upper Wensum Churches.

Great Ryburgh. Butler-Stoney, R. 1992. St Andrew's Church, Great Ryburgh. Church Tours, Burwood Hall. Drawings and notes by Freezer, D.

Gresham. Butler-Stoney, R. 1992. All Saints Church, Gresham. Church Tours, Burwood Hall.

Gresham. Anon. N.D. Churches in the Repps Deanery Welcome You. Poppyland Partnership.

Grimston. Anon. N.D. A Brief (free) guide to St. Botolph's Parish Church, Grimston, King's Lynn.

Hickling. Kemp, I. and Cornwell, T. 2005. A visitor's guide to St. Mary's Parish Church Hickling. Hickling Local History Group.

Hilborough. Anon. post 1963. The Church and Parish of All Saints, Hilborough Norfolk in the Hilborough Group of Parishes.

Hilborough. Butler-Stoney, R. 1985. All Saints Church, Hilborough. Church Tours, Burwood Hall. Drawings by Holbeach, H.

Horning. Anon. 2012. The Parish Church of St. Benedict, Horning. St Benedict's Church, Horning.

Horning. Anon. N.D. Broads & Rivers Church Staithe Guide.

Horsford. Marshall, M.A. 2008. Welcome to our Parish Church of Horsford dedicated to All Saints.

Hunworth. Linnell, C.L.S. N.D. Hunworth and Stody Churches.

Hunworth. Anon. N.D. Holt Deanery Church Trail, Diocese of Norwich. 20. Hunworth St Lawrence.

Hunworth. Hunworth PCC. 2008. St. Lawrence Hunworth. A walking guide to the building history of the church. Hunworth PCC.

Ingworth. Belton, V. N.D. St. Lawrence Church Ingworth. Illustrations by Partner, J. and Watt, D.

Kimberley. Hungate Medieval Art. N.D. Hungate Stained Glass Trails: No. 6 Kimberley, Hingham, Ashill, Great Cressingham.

Little Dunham. Butler-Stoney, R. 1997. The Church of St Margaret, Little Dunham. Church Tours, Burwood Hall. Drawing by Holbeach, H.

Little Melton. Friends of Little Melton Church. 2009. All Saints Church Little Melton.

Longham. Anon. N.D. Longham Church of St. Andrew.

Marsham. Wathen, M. N.D. Welcome to All Saint's Church Marsham.

Mileham. Anon. N.D. Churches Four. Churches around Litcham. Breckland, the Secret Heart of Norfolk. Mileham. Breckland Council, Norfolk.

Mileham. Hungate Medieval Art. N.D. Hungate Stained Glass Trails: No. 7 Mileham, South Acre, Harpley, West Rudham.

Mileham. Anon. 2004. Mileham St John the Baptist. Church Tours, Burwood Hall.

Morston. Anon. N.D. Holt Deanery Church Trail, Diocese of Norwich. 26. Morston All Saints.

Morston. Anon. N.D. All Saints Church, Morston.

Morston. Butler-Stoney, R. 1997. All Saints Church, Morston. Church Tours, Burwood Hall.

Morston. JJRW. 2011. All Saints Church Morston.

Norfolk. Churches Conservation Trust. 2011. Historic churches in Norfolk, delight in the treasures of the past. The Churches Conservation Trust.

North Pickenham. Anon. N.D. Welcome to St Andrew's. The village church in North Pickenham, Norfolk.

Old Buckenham. Butler-Stoney, R. 1994. All Saints Church, Old Buckenham.

Paston. Lorraine, H.R. N.D. St. Margaret's Church Paston and the Paston Family.

Paston. Loraine, H.R. N.D. Paston. Some notes on the Church of St. Margaret and the Paston Family.

Paston. Anon. N.D. Churches in the Repps Deanery Welcome You. Poppyland Partnership.

Plumstead. Anon. N.D. Holt Deanery Church Trail, Diocese of Norwich. 28. Plumstead St Michael & All Angels.

Plumstead. Wormald, T.J. and Durdun, J.F. 2002. A Guide to St Michael & All Angels Church Plumstead.

Redenhall. Anon. N.D. Welcome to the church of the Assumption of the Blessed Virgin Mary, Redenhall.

Rushford. Butler-Stoney, R. 2002. The Church of St John the Evangelist, Rushford. Church Tours, Burwood Hall.

Santon. Fitch, J. 2007. The Church in the Forest, St. Mary the Virgin Santon Downham, Suffolk with some notes on All Saints' Santon, Norfolk.

Santon. Anon. N.D. Santon.

Saxlingham Nethergate. Muir, M. 2004. St Mary the Virgin, Saxlingham Nethergate.

Saxlingham Nethergate. Hungate Medieval Art. N.D. Hungate Stained Glass Trails: 5. Ketteringham, Mulbarton, Saxlingham Nethergate, Shelton.

Scottow. Butler-Storey, R. N.D. Church Guide. All Saints' Church Scottow. Church Tours, Burwood Hall.

South Walsham. Groves, N.W. 1995. A Guide to St Mary's Church, South Walsham.

Southrepps. Anon. N.D. Churches in the Repps Deanery Welcome You. Poppyland Partnership.

Sparham. Butler-Stoney, R. and Sayer, M. 1993. St Mary's Church, Sparham. Church Tours, Burwood Hall.

Sparham. Sayer, M. 2014. St. Mary's Sparham. A Guide Book. Sparham Church Restoration Trust.

Stalham. Anon. N.D. The Church of St. Mary the Virgin at Stalham.

Stalham. Anon. N.D. Broads & Rivers Church Staithe Guide.

Strumpshaw. Harvey, G. and Price, N. 2007. The Church of St. Peter, Strumpshaw.

Swannington. Furness, V. N.D. Swannington St. Margaret *in* The Pilgrim Group of Churches.

Swannington. Anon. N.D. St Margaret's Church Swannington. A short guide.

Swanton Novers. Anon. N.D. Holt Deanery Church Trail, Diocese of Norwich. 34. Swanton Novers St Edmund.

Swanton Novers. Butler-Stoney, R. N.D. The Church of St. Edmund, Swanton Novers.

Swardeston. Swardeston Parochial Church Council. 2003. St Mary the Virgin, Swardeston. A brief history and guide for visitors.

Tharston. Stilgoe, L. 2011. Tharston St Mary the Virgin. Church Tours, Burwood Hall.

Thorpe Abbotts. Stilgoe, L. 2016. Thorpe Abbotts. Church Tours, Burwood Hall.

Thurlton. Anon. N.D. Welcome to the Raveningham Group of Parishes.

Thurton. Anon. N.D. Welcome to St. Ethelbert's Church Thurton.

Thurton. Anon. N.D. Three Walks starting from St. Ethelbert's Church Thurton.

Tibenham. Hawks, J. & K., Brown, K. & Pilcher, R.R. N.D. Thomas & Bertie's Guide to Tibenham Church.

Tibenham. Anon. N.D. Tibenham All Saints' Church in Churches of the Pilgrim Benefice.

Titchwell. Anon. N.D. St Mary the Virgin Titchwell.

Titchwell. Campbell, L. 2004. Church of St. Mary the Virgin Titchwell. Witley Press Ltd., Hunstanton.

Titchwell. Butler-Stoney, R. 1993. The Church of St Mary the Virgin, Titchwell. Church Tours, Burwood Hall.

Tivetshall St Margaret. Hungate Medieval Art. N.D. Hungate Rood Screen Trails: No. 9 Tivetshall St Margaret, Carleton Rode, Tacolneston, Fritton, Loddon.

Toft Monks. Glover, M.H.R. N.D. St. Margaret's Church, Toft Monks.

Toft Monks. Anon. N.D. Welcome to the Raveningham Group of Parishes.

Topcroft. Hempnall Team Council. 2010. Topcroft St Margaret in The Parish Churches of the Hempnall Group. pp 28-31.

Topcroft. Anon. N.D. Discover the Parish Churches of the Hempnall Group. Topcroft St Margaret.

Topcroft. Anon. N.D. Topcroft St Margaret.

Tunstead. Butler-Stoney, R. 2001. St Mary's Church, Tunstead. Church Tours, Burwood Hall.

Wellingham. Timpson, J. 1989. Wellingham was there. The stories behind a tiny Norfolk village and its ancient Parish Church.

Wellingham. Anon. N.D. Churches Four. Churches around Litcham. Breckland, the Secret Heart of Norfolk. Wellingham. Breckland Council, Norfolk.

Wereham. Stilgoe, L. 2006. Wereham St Margaret. Church Tours, Burwood Hall.

Wereham. D.T. 1998. Wereham Saint Margaret of Antioch. A Guide & Short History.

West Acre. Stilgoe, L. 2010. West Acre All Saints. Church Tours, Burwood Hall.

Weston Longville. Anon. N.D. A Guide to All Saints' Church, Weston Longville.

Wickhampton. Anon. N.D. The Parish Church of Saint Andrew, Wickhampton. A brief guide to our Parish Church.

Winterton on Sea. Jones, L.E. N.D. The Parish Church of Winterton-on-Sea Norfolk.

Winterton on Sea. Ling, A. 2007. The Parish Church of The Holy Trinity & All Saints Winterton-on-Sea Norfolk. A History and Guide. Revised edition.

Wiveton. Butler-Stoney, R. 1987. Wiveton St Mary the Virgin. Church Tours, Burwood Hall. Drawings by Holbeach, H.

Wiveton. Anon. N.D. Holt Deanery Church Trail, Diocese of Norwich. 39. Wiveton St Mary.

Wiveton. JNG and SMW. N.D. St Mary the Virgin Wiveton.

Wolferton. Anon. N.D. St. Peters Wolferton, Norfolk. Witley Press Ltd., Hunstanton.

Wood Dalling. Nightingale, K. N.D. St. Andrew's Church Wood Dalling.

General books on churches

Betjeman, J. 1980. Collins Guide to Parish Churches of England and Wales. Collins, London.

Cox, J.C. and Ford, C.B. 1961. Parish Churches (rev. edition). Batsford, London.

Cunnington, P. 2005. How old is that church? Marston House, Yeovil.

Fewins, C. 2010. The Church Explorer's Handbook. Canterbury Press, Norwich.

Jenkins, S. 2009. England's Thousand Best Churches. Penguin Books, London.

Jones, L.E. 1965. The Observer's Book of Old English Churches. Frederick Warne, London.

Jones, L.E. and Tricker, R. 1992. County Guide to English Churches. Countryside Books, Newbury.

Jones, L.E. 1963. What to see in a Country Church (3rd edition). Phoenix House Ltd., London.

NADFAS. 1993. Inside Churches. A Guide to Church Furnishings. NADFAS.

Smith, E., Cook, O. and Hutton, G. 1977. English Parish Churches. Book Club Associates, London.

Taylor, R. 2003. How to read a church. Rider, London.

Winn, C. 2014. I never knew that about England's Country Churches. Ebury Press, London.

Websites

Of the websites in the list, the most useful and informative regarding Norfolk churches are the British Listed Buildings, Norfolk Churches, Diocese of Norfolk and Church of England A Church Near You sites. Many, in fact most, churches now have their own website or share a benefice website. Some of these are excellent. The British History Online site is a marvellous resource, and, for Norfolk, has all 11 volumes of Francis Blomefield's monumental work of 1805 'An Essay towards a Topographical History of Norfolk' freely available for study in scanned versions. The Essay has notes on all, or nearly all, of Norfolk's churches as they were in the late C18th.

http://www.norfolkchurches.co.uk/
http://www.britishlistedbuildings.co.uk/
https://www.achurchnearyou.com/county/norfolk/

http://www.dioceseofnorwich.org/visiting/
http://www.british-history.ac.uk/
http://www.greatenglishchurches.co.uk/html/norfolk.html
http://www.english-church-architecture.net/norfolk/aa_index_norfolk.htm
http://norfolkchurchestrust.org.uk/
http://www.tournorfolk.co.uk/churches.html
http://www.visitnorfolk.co.uk/things-to-do/Churches-and-cathedrals.aspx
http://www.britainexpress.com/counties/norfolk/churches/index.htm
http://www.literarynorfolk.co.uk/norfolk_churches.htm
http://www.norfolkstainedglass.co.uk/Norfolk/home.shtm
http://www.roundtowers.org.uk/
www.crsbi.ac.uk/

Final words – the top 12

All the churches described in this book will reward your visit, all are different and have their own particular attractions. The following are among my personal favourites. They are by no means the only ones and inclusion here does not imply that they are the 'best'. Readers are encouraged to make up their own minds! My choices are in no particular order:

Weston Longville, Elsing, Castle Rising, Tibenham, Feltwell, Dickleburgh, Catfield, Great Ryburgh, Wickhampton, Paston, Chedgrave, Sparham

A last plea. Before leaving any church, please sign the visitor's book and leave a donation towards the church's funds.

Kenninghall

213